Table of Contents

Introduction 5
The Transformation of Brewing in the Industrial Age 5
The Era of Brewing Innovations 8
The Scope of This Book 11

Chapter 1: The Industrial Revolution and Brewing 15
Mechanization and Brewing 15
Steam Power and Brewery Expansion 19
Impact on Beer Quality and Consistency 23
The Emergence of Large-Scale Breweries 28

Chapter 2: The Globalization of Beer Styles 33
Pilsner, Lager, and the Rise of Pale Lagers 33
The Exportation of British Ales 37
Beer Styles Around the World 41
The Role of Global Trade and Colonialism 46

Chapter 3: Temperance and the Road to Prohibition 50
The Temperance Movement's Origins 50
Early Advocates for Abstinence 54
Anti-Saloon Leagues and Prohibitionists 59
The Impact of Temperance on Brewing 64

Chapter 4: Prohibition in America 68
The Passage of the 18th Amendment 68
The Roaring Twenties: Bootlegging and Speakeasies 73
The Effects of Prohibition on Brewing Industry Workers .. 78
Repeal and the Return of Legal Brewing 82

Chapter 5: Brewing Innovations and the Rebirth of Beer..86
Post-Prohibition Brewing Reforms 86
The Return of Small Breweries 90
Advances in Brewing Technology 94
The Birth of the Beer Can and Bottling Innovations 98

Chapter 6: Consolidation and the Rise of Beer Giants.. 103
The Growth of Mega-Breweries 103
Beer Marketing and Branding Strategies 107
The Battle for Market Dominance 111
The Impact of Consolidation on Beer Variety....................115

Chapter 7: The Craft Beer Revolution 119
The Birth of the Homebrewing Movement........................119
Microbreweries and Brewpubs 123
The Pioneers of Craft Beer 127
Craft Beer's Impact on the Brewing Landscape 131

Conclusion 135
Reflecting on the Industrial Age of Brewing 135
Prohibition's Lasting Effects 140
The Craft Beer Movement and Beyond 144

Wordbook 149

Supplementary Materials 152

Copyright © 2023 by Maxwell J. Aromano (Author)

All rights reserved. No part of this book may be reproduced or utilized in any form or by any means, electronic or mechanical, including photocopying, recording or by any information storage and retrieval system, without permission in writing from the publisher, except for brief quotations in critical articles or reviews.

The content of this book is based on various sources and is intended for educational and entertainment purposes only. While the author has made every effort to ensure the accuracy, completeness, and reliability of the information provided, the information may be subject to errors, omissions, or inaccuracies. Therefore, the author makes no warranties, express or implied, regarding the content of this book.

Readers are advised to seek the guidance of a licensed professional before attempting any techniques or actions outlined in this book. The author is not responsible for any losses, damages, or injuries that may arise from the use of information contained within. The information provided in this book is not intended to be a substitute for professional advice, and readers should not rely solely on the information presented.

By reading this book, readers acknowledge that the author is not providing legal, financial, medical, or professional advice. Any reliance on the information contained in this book is solely at the reader's own risk.

Thank you for selecting this book as a valuable source of knowledge and inspiration. Our aim is to provide you with insights and information that will enrich your understanding and enhance your personal growth. We appreciate your decision to embark on this journey of discovery with us, and we hope that this book will exceed your expectations and leave a lasting impact on your life.

Title: Beer's Industrial Era: Progress and Prohibition

Subtitle: Brewing Giants, Innovations, and the Fight Against the Dry Spell

Series: Ale Ages: Tracing the Timeline of Beer

Author: Maxwell J. Aromano

Introduction
The Transformation of Brewing in the Industrial Age

The Industrial Age marked a significant turning point in the history of beer. As the world underwent rapid industrialization and technological advancements, the brewing industry underwent a profound transformation. In this chapter, we will delve into the intricate details of how brewing evolved during this era, exploring the pivotal role played by mechanization, steam power, and the emergence of large-scale breweries. We will uncover how these changes revolutionized the production of beer, affecting its quality, consistency, and accessibility.

The Transformation of Brewing in the Industrial Age

The Industrial Revolution, which began in the late 18th century in Britain before spreading globally, brought about sweeping changes in nearly every aspect of society, including the way beer was brewed and consumed. This transformation was fueled by several key factors, each leaving an indelible mark on the brewing industry.

Mechanization and Brewing

One of the defining features of the Industrial Age was the widespread adoption of mechanization. In brewing, this meant the integration of machinery into the production process. Traditional methods of mashing, fermenting, and bottling were gradually replaced by mechanical systems that could perform these tasks with greater precision and efficiency.

Steam engines, a hallmark of the Industrial Revolution, played a pivotal role in mechanizing breweries. They provided a reliable source of power, allowing breweries to scale up production significantly. Steam power enabled the automation of various brewing processes, reducing the reliance on manual labor and setting the stage for the expansion of the brewing industry.

Steam Power and Brewery Expansion

The utilization of steam power revolutionized the scale of brewery operations. Prior to the Industrial Age, breweries were often small and localized. With the advent of steam engines, breweries could now produce beer on a much larger scale, meeting the growing demand of a rapidly urbanizing world. This expansion led to the rise of large breweries capable of supplying beer to a wider audience, both domestically and internationally.

Impact on Beer Quality and Consistency

The mechanization of brewing brought about improvements in beer quality and consistency. Traditional methods, reliant on manual labor, were prone to variations and inconsistencies. The precision of mechanized processes allowed brewers to maintain a higher level of quality control. This, in turn, contributed to the standardization of beer styles and flavors, making beer more predictable and appealing to a broader consumer base.

The Emergence of Large-Scale Breweries

As breweries grew in size and capacity, a new breed of large-scale breweries emerged. These establishments, often situated in industrial centers, became known for their ability to produce vast quantities of beer. The consolidation of resources, combined with advances in brewing technology, enabled these breweries to dominate the market and lay the groundwork for the future beer industry giants.

In this chapter, we will explore the profound impact of mechanization and steam power on brewing during the Industrial Age. We will delve into the specific innovations that revolutionized the brewing process, setting the stage for the globalization of beer styles, which we will examine in the subsequent chapter. Through this exploration, we will gain a deeper understanding of how industrialization reshaped the world of beer and set it on a trajectory that would eventually lead to the craft beer revolution of the modern era.

The Era of Brewing Innovations

The Industrial Age witnessed not only the mechanization and expansion of brewing but also a remarkable era of brewing innovations. As technology evolved and the demand for beer continued to surge, brewers and inventors embarked on a journey of creativity and experimentation. In this chapter, we will explore the remarkable period known as the "Era of Brewing Innovations," a time when brewing techniques, equipment, and ingredients underwent transformative changes. We will delve into the ingenious minds that drove these innovations and the profound impact they had on the world of beer.

The Era of Brewing Innovations represents a pivotal chapter in the history of beer. During this period, brewers and inventors sought to improve the brewing process and create unique flavors, giving rise to groundbreaking developments that would forever change the landscape of the brewing industry.

Reinventing the Brewing Process

One of the primary areas of innovation during this era was the brewing process itself. Brewers and scientists explored ways to refine the steps involved in beer production, aiming to increase efficiency and quality. This led to the development of new brewing equipment and techniques that would become the foundation of modern brewing.

Advancements in Fermentation Control

Fermentation, a critical stage in brewing, received particular attention during this period. Brewers sought to better understand the role of yeast and temperature control in the fermentation process. The advent of temperature-controlled fermentation vessels and the study of yeast strains led to more predictable and consistent results, allowing brewers to produce a wider range of beer styles with precision.

The Science of Ingredients

Innovations in brewing also extended to the ingredients used in beer production. Scientists and brewers delved into the chemistry of malt, hops, water, and yeast, unraveling the complexities of flavor and aroma compounds. This newfound knowledge empowered brewers to experiment with different combinations of ingredients, leading to the creation of diverse and distinct beer styles.

Bottling and Packaging Innovations

The era of brewing innovations also brought about significant changes in how beer was packaged and distributed. Innovations in bottling technology, including the invention of the crown cap and advancements in glass production, made it possible to bottle beer more efficiently and extend its shelf life. This, in turn, facilitated the global distribution of beer.

Pioneering Brewers and Inventors

Throughout this chapter, we will introduce you to the pioneering brewers and inventors who played a pivotal role in driving these innovations forward. Their contributions not only transformed the brewing industry but also left a lasting legacy that continues to influence brewers today.

The Impact on Beer Diversity

As we delve deeper into the innovations of this era, we will examine how these advancements contributed to the diversification of beer styles. From the emergence of lagers and ales with distinct flavor profiles to the birth of specialty and experimental brews, the Era of Brewing Innovations laid the foundation for the rich and varied world of beer that we enjoy today.

In the following sections, we will embark on a journey through time, exploring the specific innovations, individuals, and breakthroughs that defined this remarkable period in beer history. Together, we will gain a deeper appreciation for the ingenuity and creativity that have shaped the ever-evolving world of brewing.

The Scope of This Book

Before embarking on our journey through the fascinating history of beer, it's essential to understand the scope of this book. "Beer's Industrial Era: Progress and Prohibition" is a comprehensive exploration of beer's evolution, from its ancient origins to the modern craft beer revolution. In this section, we will outline what readers can expect from the pages that follow, offering a glimpse into the diverse topics, eras, and themes that will unfold as we traverse the history of this beloved beverage.

This book endeavors to provide readers with a comprehensive and engaging narrative that captures the essence of beer's rich history. To achieve this, we have divided our exploration into several distinct but interconnected chapters, each shedding light on a particular aspect of beer's journey through time.

Chapter 1: The Industrial Revolution and Brewing

In this opening chapter, we will dive into the Industrial Age and examine how mechanization, steam power, and large-scale breweries transformed the brewing landscape. From the adoption of cutting-edge technology to the impact on beer quality and consistency, we will explore how the Industrial Revolution reshaped the way beer was produced and consumed.

Chapter 2: The Globalization of Beer Styles

The second chapter delves into the globalization of beer styles, highlighting the emergence of pale lagers like Pilsner, the exportation of British ales, and the interplay of global trade and colonialism. We will discover how these developments led to the global diversity of beer styles we enjoy today.

Chapter 3: Temperance and the Road to Prohibition

This chapter unravels the history of the Temperance Movement, its origins, and its relentless pursuit of abstinence. We will delve into the early advocates for temperance, the formation of Anti-Saloon Leagues, and the profound impact of temperance on the brewing industry.

Chapter 4: Prohibition in America

Chapter 4 takes us to the tumultuous period of Prohibition in America, exploring the passage of the 18th Amendment, the Roaring Twenties characterized by bootlegging and speakeasies, and the effects of Prohibition on brewing industry workers. We will also witness the eventual repeal of Prohibition and the triumphant return of legal brewing.

Chapter 5: Brewing Innovations and the Rebirth of Beer

In this chapter, we examine the post-Prohibition brewing reforms, the resurgence of small breweries, advances in brewing technology, and the birth of the beer can and bottling innovations. We will witness the brewing industry's phoenix-like rise from the ashes of Prohibition.

Chapter 6: Consolidation and the Rise of Beer Giants

Chapter 6 delves into the growth of mega-breweries, beer marketing and branding strategies, the fierce battle for market dominance, and the impact of consolidation on beer variety. We will explore how large beer conglomerates came to dominate the global market.

Chapter 7: The Craft Beer Revolution

Our final chapter explores the birth of the homebrewing movement, the rise of microbreweries and brewpubs, and the pioneering spirit of craft beer entrepreneurs. We will delve into the lasting impact of the craft beer revolution on the brewing landscape and consumer preferences.

Conclusion

In the concluding chapter, we reflect on the Industrial Age of Brewing, the enduring effects of Prohibition, and the far-reaching influence of the craft beer movement. We consider the challenges and opportunities that lie ahead for the beer industry in the modern era.

Throughout the pages of this book, we will encounter a diverse cast of characters, from ancient brewers in Mesopotamia to contemporary craft beer pioneers. We will explore the technological advancements that revolutionized brewing, the cultural and societal shifts that shaped beer's history, and the enduring passion of those who have dedicated their lives to this remarkable beverage.

Join us on this captivating journey through time, as we raise our glasses to toast the enduring legacy of beer and the remarkable stories that have shaped its history. From the dawn of civilization to the modern craft beer renaissance, the world of beer awaits, ready to reveal its secrets, challenges, and triumphs.

Chapter 1: The Industrial Revolution and Brewing

Mechanization and Brewing

In the early 18th century, as the world was on the cusp of the Industrial Revolution, the brewing industry was on the brink of a significant transformation. The introduction of mechanization, powered by innovations like the steam engine, would forever alter the way beer was brewed. In this chapter, we delve into the profound impact of mechanization on brewing during the Industrial Age, exploring how machines revolutionized the beer production process, improved efficiency, and paved the way for the rise of large-scale breweries.

The Industrial Revolution brought about a paradigm shift in the brewing industry, as manual labor and traditional brewing methods gave way to mechanization. This transition marked the beginning of a new era in brewing, one defined by technological advancement and increased production capacity.

The Role of Machinery in Brewing

Machinery became the backbone of breweries during this period. Steam engines, driven by coal or later by other fuel sources, were at the forefront of this transformation. These engines provided a reliable source of power, replacing the human and animal labor that had been the norm in breweries for centuries.

One of the key innovations in mechanization was the steam-powered mash tun, which allowed for more efficient mashing of grains. This development significantly reduced the labor required for this critical step in brewing and resulted in more consistent and predictable outcomes.

Scaling Up Production

The adoption of steam power in brewing had a profound impact on the scale of production. Prior to mechanization, breweries were relatively small and localized, limited by the manual labor available. With the ability to harness steam power, breweries could expand their production capacity exponentially.

This shift led to the emergence of large-scale breweries, capable of producing beer on a scale never before imagined. As demand for beer grew, these breweries could meet the needs of a rapidly urbanizing population. The growth of cities and industries during the Industrial Revolution created a substantial market for beer, and mechanization enabled breweries to tap into this market more effectively.

Precision and Efficiency

Mechanization brought precision and efficiency to the brewing process. Traditional methods, dependent on manual labor, were prone to variations and inconsistencies. With the introduction of machines, brewers could control the brewing process more rigorously. This, in turn, contributed to the standardization of beer styles and flavors, making beer production more predictable and appealing to a broader consumer base.

The mechanization of brewing also led to innovations in quality control. Brewers could now monitor and adjust temperature, pressure, and other critical parameters with greater accuracy, resulting in a higher level of beer quality and consistency.

Challenges and Adaptations

While mechanization offered numerous benefits, it also presented challenges to brewers and their workforce. Some brewers resisted the transition to mechanization, fearing job losses and the loss of traditional brewing methods. Others embraced the new technology, recognizing its potential for growth and efficiency.

The transition to mechanization also required brewers to acquire new skills and knowledge. As steam engines and other machinery became integral to the brewing process, brewers had to adapt and learn to operate and maintain these complex systems.

Legacy of Mechanization

The legacy of mechanization in brewing is still evident today. The Industrial Age innovations paved the way for the brewing industry to expand, diversify, and meet the demands of a changing world. While the methods and technology have evolved since the early days of mechanization, the principles of precision, efficiency, and quality control continue to shape the modern brewing landscape.

In the pages that follow, we will further explore the impact of mechanization on brewing, from the adoption of steam power to the emergence of large-scale breweries. We will uncover the stories of inventors and visionaries who played a pivotal role in this transformation and gain a deeper understanding of how these changes set the stage for the globalization of beer styles and the development of the brewing industry as we know it today.

Steam Power and Brewery Expansion

The Industrial Revolution, a period of profound technological advancement and societal change, left an indelible mark on the brewing industry. One of its most significant contributions to brewing was the harnessing of steam power, which revolutionized the way beer was produced. In this section, we delve into the pivotal role that steam power played in the expansion of breweries during the Industrial Age, exploring how it propelled the industry into uncharted territory and paved the way for a new era of beer production.

The introduction of steam power into breweries during the Industrial Revolution was a watershed moment in the history of beer production. Steam engines, powered by coal and later other fuel sources, provided a reliable and consistent source of energy, enabling breweries to scale up their operations in unprecedented ways.

The Birth of Steam-Powered Breweries

Steam engines were first introduced to breweries in the late 18th century. The ability to generate power independently of water sources allowed breweries to be situated in more diverse locations, no longer reliant on water-driven machinery. This newfound flexibility in brewery placement contributed to the growth of urban breweries and the rapid expansion of brewing operations.

Efficiency and Consistency

One of the key advantages of steam power was its ability to deliver consistent energy, ensuring that brewing processes could be executed with precision. This newfound consistency resulted in more predictable brewing outcomes, which was a significant departure from the variable and often unpredictable nature of manual labor.

Steam-powered machinery, such as the steam-driven mash tun and steam kettles, facilitated the brewing process, reducing the time required for mashing, boiling, and other essential brewing steps. These advancements significantly improved efficiency and allowed brewers to produce larger quantities of beer in less time.

The Rise of Large-Scale Breweries

As breweries adopted steam power, they saw their production capacities soar. The ability to brew beer at a much larger scale was particularly appealing in rapidly growing urban centers, where the demand for beer was on the rise. Large-scale breweries emerged as industry leaders, capable of supplying vast quantities of beer to both local and international markets.

The adoption of steam power led to the consolidation of brewing operations. Smaller breweries struggled to compete with the efficiency and production capacity of their larger counterparts. Consequently, many smaller breweries were absorbed by or merged with larger ones, further fueling the expansion of the brewing giants of the era.

Transportation and Distribution

Steam power not only transformed the brewing process but also revolutionized the transportation and distribution of beer. Steam-driven locomotives and ships allowed breweries to distribute their products more widely and efficiently. This expansion of distribution networks played a crucial role in making beer more accessible to consumers across different regions.

Challenges and Innovations

The transition to steam power was not without its challenges. Brewers and engineers had to adapt to new technologies and learn to operate and maintain steam engines. Additionally, the use of coal as a fuel source presented environmental and health concerns, leading to ongoing efforts to improve safety and efficiency.

Legacy of Steam Power

The legacy of steam power in brewing is still evident in the modern brewing industry. While the technology itself has evolved, the principles of efficiency, consistency, and scalability introduced during the Industrial Revolution continue to shape how beer is produced today.

In the pages that follow, we will explore the enduring impact of steam power on brewing during the Industrial Age. We will also uncover the stories of the pioneers who harnessed this revolutionary energy source, propelling the brewing industry into an era of expansion and innovation. Steam power was not merely a technological advancement; it was a catalyst for the globalization of beer styles and the transformation of brewing from a local craft to a global industry.

Impact on Beer Quality and Consistency

The Industrial Revolution brought sweeping changes to the brewing industry, from the adoption of mechanization to the harnessing of steam power. Among its significant impacts, the revolution played a pivotal role in enhancing the quality and consistency of beer production. In this section, we delve into how these changes transformed the brewing process, ushering in an era of beer that was more reliable, standardized, and palatable to a broader consumer base.

The quest for greater quality and consistency in beer production was a driving force behind many of the technological innovations of the Industrial Revolution. Here, we explore how these changes influenced the sensory and qualitative aspects of beer, from its flavor and aroma to its shelf life and appeal.

Standardization of Brewing Processes

Before the Industrial Revolution, brewing was a largely manual and artisanal endeavor. Recipes and methods varied widely from one brewery to another, and even from batch to batch. This lack of standardization meant that the quality and characteristics of beer were often unpredictable.

With the adoption of mechanization and steam power, breweries gained the ability to standardize various aspects of the brewing process. Precise temperature control, automated stirring, and consistent mashing and fermentation times became possible. This newfound control allowed brewers to produce beer with a more uniform flavor profile and overall quality.

Temperature Control and Fermentation

One of the critical factors influencing beer quality is fermentation temperature. Prior to the Industrial Revolution, maintaining a stable and controlled fermentation temperature was a significant challenge. Brewers relied on ambient conditions, which could vary greatly depending on the season and location.

Steam-powered cooling systems and temperature-controlled fermentation vessels revolutionized this aspect of brewing. Brewers could now ferment beer at consistent temperatures, resulting in cleaner and more predictable fermentation outcomes. This level of control was particularly important for lager brewing, where lower temperatures were required.

Quality Ingredients and Brewing Hygiene

Another aspect of beer quality was the sourcing of consistent and high-quality ingredients. The Industrial Revolution facilitated improvements in ingredient sourcing and processing. For example, advances in transportation and logistics allowed breweries to access a wider range of malt varieties and hop strains from different regions.

Additionally, the growing understanding of brewing chemistry and microbiology led to advancements in brewing hygiene. Brewers gained insights into yeast management, the importance of clean and sanitized equipment, and the prevention of off-flavors. These developments played a crucial role in enhancing beer quality and consistency.

Quality Control and Sensory Evaluation

Quality control measures became more prevalent during this period. Breweries implemented tasting panels and sensory evaluation processes to ensure that each batch of beer met the desired flavor and aroma standards. These panels helped identify and address any off-flavors or inconsistencies in the final product.

Shelf Life and Distribution

Improvements in beer quality also extended to its shelf life. With better quality control and packaging innovations, such as the crown cap, beer could be preserved and transported more effectively. This was particularly important as breweries began distributing their products over longer distances.

Consumer Expectations and Preferences

As beer quality and consistency improved, consumer expectations evolved. Beer drinkers came to expect a more standardized product, and breweries that could deliver on this promise found success in the market. The growing middle class and urbanization further fueled the demand for reliable and consistent beer.

Challenges and Criticisms

Despite these advancements, there were criticisms and challenges associated with the pursuit of quality and consistency. Some argued that the focus on uniformity led to a homogenization of beer styles, with traditional regional variations diminishing. Additionally, concerns were raised about the potential loss of unique flavors and characteristics that were present in artisanal and local brews.

Legacy of Quality and Consistency

The legacy of the Industrial Revolution's impact on beer quality and consistency is still evident today. The principles of quality control, standardized processes, and sensory evaluation continue to shape modern brewing practices. While craft breweries often celebrate diversity and experimentation, the foundation laid during this era has contributed to the overall quality and reliability of beer available to consumers worldwide.

In the following sections, we will continue our exploration of the Industrial Revolution's influence on brewing, delving into the emergence of large-scale breweries and their role in shaping the modern beer industry. We will uncover the stories of pioneers who navigated these changes, laying the groundwork for the globalization of beer styles and the dynamic brewing landscape we know today.

The Emergence of Large-Scale Breweries

The Industrial Revolution not only introduced mechanization and steam power to brewing but also gave rise to the emergence of large-scale breweries. These breweries, powered by innovation and efficiency, played a crucial role in reshaping the brewing industry during the 18th and 19th centuries. In this section, we explore the factors that led to the growth of large-scale breweries, the technologies that enabled their expansion, and the profound impact they had on the beer landscape.

As the Industrial Revolution gained momentum, so did the expansion of breweries on an unprecedented scale. The shift towards large-scale production marked a significant departure from the smaller, localized breweries of the past.

Factors Driving Expansion

Several factors converged to fuel the emergence of large-scale breweries during this era:

1. Urbanization: The rapid growth of cities led to an increased demand for beer, as more people moved to urban centers for work and opportunity. Large-scale breweries were strategically positioned to supply these growing urban populations.

2. Advances in Transportation: Improved transportation networks, including railways and canals, made it easier to distribute beer over longer distances. Large breweries could take advantage of these networks to reach broader markets.

3. Efficiency of Mechanization: The adoption of mechanization and steam power allowed breweries to produce beer more efficiently and at a lower cost per barrel. This efficiency made large-scale production economically viable.

4. Standardization: Mechanization and the use of steam power led to greater standardization in brewing processes. This meant that large breweries could produce beer with consistent quality and characteristics, appealing to a broader consumer base.

Technological Innovations

Large-scale breweries were at the forefront of technological innovation, incorporating cutting-edge machinery and equipment into their operations:

1. Steam Engines: The use of steam engines powered the machinery that replaced manual labor. This enabled breweries to automate various aspects of the brewing process, significantly increasing production capacity.

2. Fermentation Control: Temperature-controlled fermentation vessels allowed for more precise and reliable fermentation. Brewers could now produce lagers and ales with consistent flavor profiles.

3. Bottling Innovations: Innovations in bottling technology, such as the crown cap, made it possible to package beer more efficiently, extending its shelf life and enabling wider distribution.

4. Quality Control: Large breweries implemented quality control measures, including sensory evaluation and tasting panels, to ensure that each batch of beer met specific quality standards.

The Brewing Giants of the Industrial Age

The emergence of large-scale breweries led to the formation of brewing giants that dominated the industry. Some of these breweries became household names and played a central role in shaping beer markets:

1. Bass & Co. Brewery: Located in Burton upon Trent, England, Bass & Co. became one of the largest and most prominent breweries of its time. It was known for its pale ales and its innovative use of Burton well water.

2. Anheuser-Busch: Founded in St. Louis, Missouri, USA, Anheuser-Busch was a pioneer in the use of pasteurization and refrigerated railcars. The brewery's

flagship brand, Budweiser, became a symbol of American brewing.

3. Pilsner Urquell Brewery: Located in Plzeň, Czech Republic, Pilsner Urquell introduced the world to the pale lager style. Its success paved the way for the global popularity of lagers.

4. Guinness Brewery: Based in Dublin, Ireland, Guinness is renowned for its stout. It embraced technological advancements, such as the use of nitrogen and modern packaging methods.

Impact on Beer Variety

While large-scale breweries were instrumental in meeting the growing demand for beer, they also faced criticism for their role in standardizing beer styles and diminishing regional variations. Critics argued that the focus on efficiency and consistency led to the homogenization of beer.

However, it's important to note that large breweries did not entirely extinguish diversity in beer. They still produced a range of beer styles, and their ability to reach larger markets introduced consumers to a wider variety of options than ever before.

Legacy of Large-Scale Breweries

The legacy of large-scale breweries is evident in the modern beer industry. While craft breweries celebrate diversity and innovation, large breweries continue to produce a significant portion of the world's beer. The efficiency and quality control practices developed during the Industrial Revolution continue to shape brewing today, ensuring that beer remains a globally enjoyed beverage with consistent quality.

In the chapters that follow, we will further explore the impact of the Industrial Revolution on brewing, including the globalization of beer styles and the challenges posed by temperance movements and prohibition. We will uncover the stories of the pioneers who navigated these changes, leaving a lasting mark on the history of beer.

Chapter 2: The Globalization of Beer Styles
Pilsner, Lager, and the Rise of Pale Lagers

As the Industrial Revolution transformed brewing, it also laid the foundation for the globalization of beer styles. This chapter explores the emergence of pale lagers, with a special focus on the iconic Pilsner and the broader category of lagers. We will delve into the technological innovations, cultural influences, and global trade networks that propelled the rise of these light and crisp beers, forever altering the world's beer landscape.

The 19th century witnessed a dramatic shift in beer styles, as the world was introduced to the refreshing, golden-hued brews that would come to define the modern beer experience. This section explores the origins of pale lagers, the story behind Pilsner, and the global impact of these new beer styles.

The Birth of the Pale Lager

Before the emergence of pale lagers, the beer landscape was dominated by ales, porters, and stouts, which were typically dark and heavy in character. The development of pale lagers marked a revolutionary departure from this tradition.

Pilsner: A Beer Revolution

The town of Plzeň (Pilsen) in the Czech Republic is credited with pioneering the pale lager style. In 1842, the citizens of Plzeň came together to create a beer that would challenge the conventions of the time. The result was Pilsner Urquell, a clear, golden beer characterized by its crispness and balance.

We explore the story behind Pilsner Urquell, from the city's determination to brew a better beer to the contributions of innovators like Josef Groll. The introduction of bottom-fermentation using lager yeast, coupled with the use of pale malt and Saaz hops, created a beer that set a new standard for clarity, flavor, and drinkability.

Lagers Take the World by Storm

The success of Pilsner Urquell ignited a global fascination with pale lagers. Breweries across Europe and beyond sought to replicate the style, giving rise to a wide array of lagers. These beers were characterized by their clean, crisp taste, and the lagering process—cold storage for extended periods—contributed to their clarity and mellow character.

German Lagers and the Reinheitsgebot

Germany, with its rich brewing tradition, played a significant role in the proliferation of lagers. German brewers developed their own interpretations of the pale lager, often adhering to the Reinheitsgebot (Beer Purity Law), which dictated the use of only four ingredients: water, malt, hops, and yeast. This commitment to quality and simplicity influenced the development of German lagers, such as Helles and Märzen.

The Global Spread of Lager Brewing

As trade networks expanded and immigrants carried their brewing traditions to new lands, lager brewing spread across the globe. European immigrants brought their lager recipes to the United States, leading to the establishment of American lager traditions. Brewers in other countries, including Mexico, Brazil, and Japan, also embraced the pale lager style.

Challenges and Adaptations

The rise of pale lagers was not without its challenges. Brewers had to adapt to new ingredients, such as pale malt and noble hops, which were distinct from the materials used in traditional ale brewing. Lager yeast, which ferments at cooler temperatures, required changes to fermentation practices and equipment.

Lager in the Modern World

Today, pale lagers, including Pilsner-style beers, Helles, and other regional varieties, remain some of the most widely consumed beers globally. They are celebrated for their clean, refreshing taste and versatility. Yet, even within the category of lagers, there is a remarkable diversity of flavors and styles.

Innovation and Tradition

While pale lagers adhere to a traditional set of ingredients and brewing methods, modern craft brewers continue to innovate within this category. They experiment with hop varieties, yeast strains, and aging techniques to create unique and exciting lager experiences that pay homage to tradition while pushing the boundaries of flavor.

Conclusion

The rise of pale lagers, with Pilsner as its shining star, marked a transformative moment in the history of beer. These beers captured the imagination of consumers around the world and became symbols of quality and consistency. In the pages that follow, we will explore how this globalization of beer styles, fueled by technological innovation and cultural exchange, reshaped the beer landscape and set the stage for the diverse array of styles available to beer enthusiasts today.

The Exportation of British Ales

The Industrial Revolution not only gave birth to pale lagers like Pilsner but also led to the exportation of British ales. This chapter delves into the story of how British ales, with their rich history and diverse styles, made their way to international markets, influencing beer traditions around the world. We explore the factors that fueled this exportation and the enduring legacy of British ales in the global beer landscape.

The Exportation of British Ales

While the emergence of pale lagers was a defining moment in brewing history, British ales played an equally crucial role in shaping the global beer scene during the 19th and early 20th centuries.

The British Ale Tradition

British ales have a storied history dating back centuries. The United Kingdom, with its diverse regions and brewing practices, was known for producing a wide range of ales, each with its unique characteristics:

1. Bitter Ales: Characterized by their balanced malt and hop profiles, bitter ales were a staple of British pubs and enjoyed for their sessionable nature.

2. Porters and Stouts: These dark ales, known for their roasted malt flavors, were especially popular in London. The

invention of stout and the birth of the Guinness brewery in Ireland also played a significant role in this category.

3. India Pale Ales (IPAs): Originally brewed for export to British troops stationed in India, IPAs gained fame for their bold hoppy character and higher alcohol content, which helped preserve the beer during long sea voyages.

4. Scottish Ales: Scotland had its own brewing traditions, producing ales like Scotch ales and wee heavy, which were known for their malt-forward profiles.

The Role of the British Empire

The British Empire, at its zenith during the 19th century, played a pivotal role in the exportation of British ales. British soldiers, merchants, and colonists stationed around the world developed a taste for the ales of their homeland. Brewers saw the potential to cater to this growing market, and British ales began their journey across the seas.

Exporting to the Colonies

British ales found their way to the far reaches of the British Empire, from India to Africa, the Caribbean, and beyond. Local breweries often sprang up in these colonies, producing ales that were inspired by British traditions but adapted to local ingredients and tastes.

The Influence of Brewing Technology

The Industrial Revolution had a profound impact on brewing technology, making it easier to brew and transport ales over long distances. Innovations in bottling, transportation, and refrigeration allowed British ales to maintain their quality and flavor even when far from home.

The Rise of the Export Market

The demand for British ales grew steadily, and breweries adapted to meet this demand. Export versions of popular ales, such as India Pale Ales designed for the journey to India, were brewed to be more robust and hoppy to withstand the rigors of long voyages.

Local Adaptations and Variations

As British ales traveled the world, they often underwent adaptations and variations to suit local tastes and ingredients. In many cases, these adaptations resulted in unique beer styles that blended British brewing traditions with local flavors and brewing techniques.

The Legacy of British Ales

The exportation of British ales left a lasting legacy on the global beer landscape. Many countries developed their own beer traditions inspired by British ales, leading to the creation of styles like American Pale Ale (APA) and Australian Sparkling Ale, which are indebted to their British predecessors.

Modern Resurgence and Craft Brewing

In recent decades, there has been a resurgence of interest in traditional British ales, both in their classic forms and as sources of inspiration for modern craft brewers. Breweries around the world pay homage to the British ale tradition by brewing bitters, porters, stouts, and IPAs that celebrate the flavors and history of these iconic styles.

Conclusion

The exportation of British ales was a significant chapter in the history of beer globalization. It showcased the adaptability of brewing traditions, the influence of cultural exchange, and the enduring appeal of these classic beer styles. In the chapters that follow, we will continue our exploration of the globalization of beer styles, including the role of global trade and colonialism in shaping the diversity of beers enjoyed worldwide.

Beer Styles Around the World

In the wake of the Industrial Revolution, beer styles from various parts of the world began to intermingle and influence each other. This chapter explores the diversification of beer styles around the world during the 19th and early 20th centuries. From the rich brewing traditions of Europe to the emergence of unique beer styles in far-flung corners of the globe, we trace the global evolution of beer and its impact on cultural exchange.

The globalization of beer styles was a complex and dynamic process, with each region contributing its unique traditions and innovations to the global tapestry of beer.

European Beer Traditions

Europe was a crucible of beer diversity during this era, with each nation producing its own distinct styles. Some highlights include:

1. Belgium: Known for its Trappist ales, lambics, and saisons, Belgium boasted a rich tapestry of beer styles that celebrated wild fermentation, complex flavors, and unique ingredients.

2. Germany: Home to renowned lagers, wheat beers, and bocks, Germany's beer culture was defined by its adherence to the Reinheitsgebot (Beer Purity Law) and its regional brewing traditions.

3. England: Beyond ales and stouts, England saw the emergence of unique styles like barleywines, old ales, and mild ales, each with its own historical and regional significance.

4. Ireland: The birthplace of the dry stout, Ireland's Guinness and other stouts made their mark globally, while Irish red ales and other styles added to the country's beer diversity.

Cultural Exchange and Innovation

As beer traveled across borders, it influenced and was influenced by the cultures it encountered. Trade routes, immigration, and colonialism played pivotal roles in shaping the global beer landscape.

The Americas

North and South America witnessed the convergence of European beer traditions with indigenous ingredients and brewing practices. This fusion resulted in unique beer styles:

1. American Ale Traditions: American Pale Ale (APA), California Common, and Cream Ale emerged in the United States, blending European influences with American innovation.

2. Mexican Lager: The influence of German immigrants in Mexico led to the creation of Mexican lagers,

with brands like Corona and Modelo becoming internationally recognized.

3. South American Beer Diversity: Countries like Brazil and Argentina developed their own beer traditions, featuring styles like Brazilian malzbier and Argentinian red ales.

Asia and the Pacific

Beer styles in Asia and the Pacific region also evolved, reflecting a blend of indigenous ingredients and European brewing techniques:

1. Japanese Lager: Japan embraced lagers, with major breweries like Sapporo and Asahi producing clean, crisp lagers that became popular both domestically and internationally.

2. Chinese Beer Culture: China's beer market exploded in the 20th century, featuring pale lagers and, more recently, craft beer innovations.

3. Australia and New Zealand: These countries saw the rise of unique styles like Australian Sparkling Ale and New Zealand Pilsner, influenced by British and German traditions.

Africa and the Middle East

Beer traditions in Africa and the Middle East also flourished, with indigenous ingredients and cultural practices shaping regional beer styles:

1. South African Beer: South Africa's beer landscape includes styles like African lagers and sorghum-based beers that celebrate local ingredients and brewing methods.

2. Middle Eastern Traditions: Traditional Middle Eastern beer-like beverages like sahti and tej continue to be produced, often incorporating spices and honey.

Global Beer Exchange and Innovation

The globalization of beer styles was a two-way street. As beers from different regions influenced each other, new hybrid styles emerged, showcasing the creativity and adaptability of brewers worldwide:

1. India Pale Ale (IPA): Originally brewed in England for export to India, the IPA has become a global sensation with various substyles like American IPA, Double IPA, and New England IPA.

2. Baltic Porter: This style emerged from the blending of British porter traditions with the lagering techniques of northern Europe.

3. Fusion Beers: Brewers continue to experiment with cross-cultural and fusion styles, creating unique and unexpected flavor combinations.

Conclusion

The globalization of beer styles reflects the interconnectedness of our world and the spirit of cultural exchange that defines beer culture. It celebrates the diverse range of flavors, ingredients, and traditions that contribute to the ever-evolving global beer scene. In the chapters that follow, we will explore how global trade and colonialism further shaped the brewing landscape, as well as the challenges posed by temperance movements and prohibition.

The Role of Global Trade and Colonialism

The global reach of beer styles during the 19th and early 20th centuries was significantly influenced by global trade and colonialism. In this section, we explore the pivotal role played by trade networks, colonial expansion, and the movement of people in the dissemination of beer styles across borders. We delve into how these factors shaped the international beer landscape and contributed to the diversity of brewing traditions worldwide.

Global trade and colonialism were two powerful forces that facilitated the exchange of beer styles and brewing traditions among nations and regions. These interconnected processes had a profound impact on the development and diversification of beer around the world.

Trade Routes and Beer Exportation

Trade routes, whether by sea or land, were vital channels for the exportation of beer styles. Breweries in Europe, particularly in the United Kingdom, Germany, and Belgium, were well-positioned to take advantage of these trade routes to supply beer to various parts of the world.

Colonial Expansion and the Spread of Beer

European colonial powers established outposts and colonies in regions across Africa, Asia, and the Americas.

Along with their cultural, political, and economic influence, they introduced beer to these new territories.

Beer as a Commodity of Trade

Beer became a valuable commodity in colonial trade. Brewers and merchants recognized the potential for exporting beer to colonial markets, and breweries were often established in or near colonial outposts to meet the demand of European settlers.

Adaptation to Local Ingredients

Brewers in colonial regions often had to adapt to local ingredients and brewing conditions. This adaptation led to the development of unique beer styles that incorporated indigenous grains, fruits, spices, and other ingredients.

The Influence of Colonial Powers

Different colonial powers influenced beer traditions in their respective colonies:

1. British Influence: British colonialists brought ales, stouts, and bitters to many parts of the world, leading to the creation of local adaptations and hybrid styles.

2. German Influence: German immigrants and colonial administrators played a role in introducing lagers and wheat beers to colonies, particularly in South America and Africa.

3. Belgian Influence: Belgian ales and lambics found their way into colonies, influencing the development of beer styles in regions such as the Belgian Congo.

Indigenous Brewing Traditions

In some cases, indigenous brewing traditions were already well-established in colonial regions. The coexistence of local brewing practices and European beer traditions resulted in a rich tapestry of beer styles:

1. Sorghum and Millet Beers: African countries often brewed beers from sorghum, millet, or other local grains, which were adapted to European brewing methods.

2. Chicha and Pulque: Indigenous beers like chicha (made from maize) in South America and pulque (fermented agave sap) in Mexico coexisted with European styles.

Global Distribution of Ingredients

Global trade not only facilitated the spread of beer styles but also contributed to the worldwide availability of brewing ingredients. Hops, malt, and yeast from different regions found their way into breweries worldwide, influencing the flavor profiles of beers.

Challenges and Conflicts

While global trade and colonialism contributed to the exchange of beer styles, they were not without challenges.

Conflicts and disputes over trade routes and resources sometimes disrupted beer production and distribution.

The Enduring Legacy

The legacy of global trade and colonialism in the world of beer is evident today. Many countries continue to produce beer styles that reflect the influence of colonial powers or the fusion of indigenous and European brewing traditions. These styles celebrate the diversity of flavors and ingredients that have enriched the global beer landscape.

Conclusion

Global trade and colonialism were instrumental in the globalization of beer styles, creating a dynamic and interconnected brewing world. The exchange of ideas, ingredients, and techniques led to the development of unique beer traditions that endure to this day. In the following chapters, we will explore the impact of temperance movements, prohibition, and brewing innovations on the evolving beer landscape.

Chapter 3: Temperance and the Road to Prohibition
The Temperance Movement's Origins

As we delve into the chapter on the Temperance Movement and the journey towards Prohibition, it is essential to begin by understanding the origins of the Temperance Movement. This section explores the early roots of temperance advocacy, tracing its emergence in various societies and the motivations that fueled the movement's growth.

The Temperance Movement, which would later gain momentum and lead to Prohibition in many parts of the world, had its beginnings in the 19th century. To comprehend the movement's rise and influence, we must first explore its origins:

Early Concerns About Alcohol Consumption

Alcohol consumption has been a part of human history for millennia, but concerns about its effects on individuals and society began to surface more prominently in the 18th and 19th centuries. Several factors contributed to these concerns:

1. Industrialization: The rise of industrialization brought changes to work and living conditions, with alcohol often seen as a means of coping with the stresses and challenges of urban life.

2. Urbanization: Increasing urbanization led to higher population densities and social problems, some of which were attributed to excessive drinking.

3. Public Health Concerns: Concerns about the physical and mental health effects of alcohol consumption started to gain attention among medical professionals.

Emergence of Early Temperance Societies

The early Temperance Movement was characterized by the formation of local temperance societies and the publication of tracts and pamphlets advocating for moderation or abstinence from alcohol. Key developments include:

1. The Scottish Example: In the late 18th century, Scotland saw the formation of temperance societies that promoted sobriety and encouraged individuals to sign temperance pledges.

2. Religious Influence: Many early temperance advocates were motivated by religious convictions. Evangelical Christians, in particular, played a significant role in promoting abstinence from alcohol.

3. Advocacy through Literature: The publication of books and pamphlets, such as "The Drunkard's Progress" by Nathaniel Currier, used vivid imagery to depict the detrimental effects of alcohol on individuals and families.

Temperance as a Social Reform Movement

As the Temperance Movement evolved, it became intertwined with broader social reform efforts. Temperance advocates saw alcohol as a root cause of various societal ills and sought to address issues such as poverty, crime, and domestic violence through temperance.

International Influence and Expansion

The Temperance Movement was not limited to one country or region. It gained momentum in various parts of the world, with each nation adapting the movement to its own social and cultural context:

1. The United States: The American Temperance Society, founded in 1826, became a prominent early advocate for temperance. The movement gained widespread support, leading to the formation of numerous local and state temperance societies.

2. Ireland: Ireland saw the emergence of the Irish Temperance Movement, with the Catholic Church playing a significant role in promoting abstinence.

3. Canada: The Canadian temperance movement mirrored developments in the United States, with the goal of reducing alcohol consumption and its societal impact.

4. United Kingdom: The United Kingdom witnessed the growth of temperance societies, which advocated for

moderation or abstinence from alcohol. Influential figures like Thomas Cook also incorporated temperance values into travel and tourism.

Political Engagement and Legislation

As the Temperance Movement gained strength, it increasingly turned to political action to achieve its goals. Advocates pushed for legislation to restrict or ban the sale and consumption of alcohol, setting the stage for the era of Prohibition in many countries.

Conclusion

The origins of the Temperance Movement can be traced back to early concerns about the effects of alcohol on individuals and society. What began as local societies and grassroots efforts evolved into a global movement with a significant impact on the laws and regulations surrounding alcohol. In the following sections, we will explore the Temperance Movement's growth, the rise of Anti-Saloon Leagues and Prohibitionists, and the profound impact of temperance on the brewing industry.

Early Advocates for Abstinence

In the journey towards Prohibition, early advocates for abstinence played a pivotal role in shaping the Temperance Movement. This section delves into the lives and motivations of individuals who championed the cause of abstinence from alcohol during the 19th century. Their efforts laid the foundation for the broader Temperance Movement and the eventual push for Prohibition.

The call for abstinence from alcohol gained momentum in the 19th century, thanks to the dedication and passion of individuals who believed in the virtues of sobriety. These early advocates for abstinence emerged from diverse backgrounds and brought their unique perspectives to the Temperance Movement:

1. The Role of Religious Leaders

Dr. Thomas Sewell - Dr. Sewell, a Methodist minister in the United States, was one of the earliest religious leaders to promote abstinence from alcohol. He argued that alcohol was a threat to moral and spiritual well-being. His sermons and writings on temperance influenced many within the Methodist denomination.

John Wesley - The founder of Methodism, John Wesley, condemned excessive drinking and encouraged moderation. His teachings had a lasting impact on

Methodists and contributed to the development of temperance principles within the denomination.

2. Early Temperance Pioneers

Rev. Lyman Beecher - A prominent Presbyterian minister, Beecher was a leading advocate for abstinence from alcohol. His influential sermons, such as the "Six Sermons on Intemperance," sparked discussions about the moral implications of alcohol consumption.

Dr. Benjamin Rush - Dr. Rush, a physician and signer of the Declaration of Independence, was one of the first medical professionals to speak out against alcohol. He wrote essays and gave lectures on the physical and mental health consequences of excessive drinking.

3. The Women's Temperance Crusade

Annie Wittenmyer - Annie Wittenmyer was a driving force behind the Women's Temperance Crusade, a grassroots movement that called for the closure of saloons and the promotion of abstinence. Wittenmyer and other women organized prayer meetings, marches, and protests to combat the influence of alcohol in their communities.

Eliza Jane Thompson - Thompson, a Quaker, was another key figure in the Women's Temperance Crusade. She organized the first crusade in Ohio, leading women in prayer and peaceful protests outside saloons. Thompson's activism inspired similar movements in other states.

4. Abolitionists and Temperance

Frederick Douglass - The famed abolitionist Frederick Douglass was also an advocate for temperance. He recognized the parallels between the struggles against slavery and excessive drinking, emphasizing the importance of self-control and personal liberty.

Sojourner Truth - Sojourner Truth, an African American abolitionist and women's rights activist, joined the temperance movement as well. Her speeches and writings promoted abstinence and the empowerment of marginalized communities through sobriety.

5. International Figures

Father Mathew - Known as the "Apostle of Temperance," Father Mathew was an Irish Catholic priest who gained fame for his temperance work in Ireland and the United States. He administered temperance pledges and inspired millions to abstain from alcohol.

Carrie Nation - While often associated with the later period of temperance agitation, Carrie Nation began her activism in the late 19th century. She gained notoriety for her "hatchetations," where she entered saloons and smashed liquor bottles to protest alcohol sales.

6. The Formation of Early Temperance Societies

Various temperance societies, such as the Washington Temperance Society and the American Temperance Society, were founded by individuals who sought to promote sobriety and abstinence. These organizations held meetings, published literature, and encouraged members to take temperance pledges.

7. The Global Reach of Early Advocates

The message of abstinence spread beyond the United States, with temperance advocates like William Booth (founder of the Salvation Army) in the United Kingdom, and organizations like the Band of Hope, promoting temperance principles among children.

Impact on the Temperance Movement

The efforts of these early advocates laid the groundwork for the broader Temperance Movement. Their moral, medical, and social arguments against alcohol consumption resonated with many, leading to the formation of local temperance societies, the publication of temperance literature, and the eventual push for legal restrictions on alcohol.

Conclusion

Early advocates for abstinence from alcohol played a vital role in the emergence and growth of the Temperance

Movement. Their diverse backgrounds and motivations contributed to the multifaceted nature of the movement, which would eventually lead to significant societal changes, including the push for Prohibition. In the following sections, we will explore the Anti-Saloon Leagues, the effects of Prohibition on the brewing industry, and the eventual repeal of Prohibition.

Anti-Saloon Leagues and Prohibitionists

In the journey towards Prohibition, the Temperance Movement gained considerable momentum through the efforts of Anti-Saloon Leagues and Prohibitionists. This section explores the rise of these organized movements and the individuals who played pivotal roles in advocating for the complete ban on the sale and consumption of alcoholic beverages.

As the Temperance Movement evolved, it saw the emergence of more organized and politically active groups dedicated to achieving the goal of Prohibition. The Anti-Saloon Leagues and Prohibitionists would become powerful forces in the push for legal restrictions on alcohol:

1. Formation of Anti-Saloon Leagues

The Ohio Example - The formation of the Anti-Saloon League in Ohio in 1893 marked a significant turning point. Led by influential figures like Wayne Wheeler and Howard Hyde Russell, the league aimed to unite various temperance organizations and wield political influence at the state and national levels.

Political Engagement - The Anti-Saloon League adopted a sophisticated approach to lobbying and political activism. It targeted key political positions and supported candidates who pledged to enact stricter alcohol regulations.

The Role of Wayne Wheeler - Wayne Wheeler, known as the "dry boss" of the Prohibition era, was a driving force behind the Anti-Saloon League. His strategic brilliance and unwavering commitment to the cause made him a formidable figure in the fight for Prohibition.

2. Prohibitionists and Their Advocacy

Frances Willard - Frances Willard, a prominent leader in the Women's Christian Temperance Union (WCTU), played a significant role in advancing the cause of Prohibition. She emphasized the impact of alcohol on women and families and used her position to garner support for temperance legislation.

Carrie Nation - While known for her direct-action approach to temperance, Carrie Nation also advocated for the complete abolition of alcohol. Her unapologetic stance and headline-grabbing actions brought attention to the cause.

The Influence of Religious Groups - Religious denominations, including Methodists, Baptists, and Presbyterians, played a crucial role in supporting Prohibition. Many church leaders and congregations actively promoted temperance and abstinence from alcohol.

3. The Push for Constitutional Amendments

The 18th Amendment - In the United States, the culmination of the Prohibition movement was the ratification of the 18th Amendment to the Constitution in 1919. This amendment prohibited the manufacture, sale, and transportation of alcoholic beverages.

The Role of Women - Women's organizations, including the WCTU, were instrumental in rallying support for the 18th Amendment. Their dedication to the cause and grassroots organizing efforts helped secure its passage.

4. International Impact

Global Prohibition Movements - The Prohibition movement was not confined to the United States. Temperance advocates in countries such as Canada, Australia, and the United Kingdom also pushed for alcohol restrictions, with varying degrees of success.

Effects on Brewing and Industry

Impact on Breweries - The Prohibition movement had a profound impact on the brewing industry. Many breweries either closed down, shifted to producing non-alcoholic beverages, or went underground to produce illicit alcohol.

The Temperance Argument - Prohibitionists argued that alcohol consumption led to social problems, including poverty, domestic violence, and crime. They believed that the complete ban on alcohol would lead to a more morally upright society.

Enforcement Challenges - The enforcement of Prohibition proved challenging, as illegal alcohol production and distribution networks thrived. The era saw the rise of organized crime and speakeasies.

5. The Repeal of Prohibition

The 21st Amendment - The 21st Amendment to the U.S. Constitution, ratified in 1933, repealed the 18th Amendment and ended Prohibition. The repeal marked a significant shift in public sentiment and the recognition of the limitations of alcohol bans.

Legacy and Lessons

Continued Advocacy - The temperance movement and Prohibition left a lasting legacy. Advocacy groups such as Mothers Against Drunk Driving (MADD) continue to work towards reducing drunk driving and alcohol-related harm.

Balancing Regulation - The Prohibition era highlighted the importance of finding a balance between regulating alcohol and respecting individual liberties. Modern alcohol regulations in many countries reflect this ongoing debate.

Conclusion

The rise of Anti-Saloon Leagues and Prohibitionists marked a decisive phase in the Temperance Movement's journey towards Prohibition. Their organized efforts, political engagement, and dedication to the cause led to significant legal changes and the prohibition of alcohol in many countries. In the subsequent sections, we will explore the effects of Prohibition on society, the brewing industry, and the eventual return to legal alcohol consumption.

The Impact of Temperance on Brewing

As we explore the Temperance Movement and the path to Prohibition, it's essential to understand the profound impact that temperance advocacy had on the brewing industry. This section delves into how the Temperance Movement influenced brewing practices, shaped the alcohol market, and ultimately led to significant changes in the industry.

The Temperance Movement's goal of reducing or eliminating alcohol consumption had far-reaching consequences for the brewing industry. Breweries and brewers found themselves at the center of the debate over alcohol's role in society:

1. The Decline of Traditional Beer Styles

Effects of Abstinence Advocacy - The Temperance Movement promoted abstinence from alcohol, including beer. This advocacy led to a decline in the consumption of traditional beer styles, such as ales and stouts, which were seen as alcoholic beverages.

Shift Toward Low-Alcohol Options - Brewers responded to the call for moderation by producing low-alcohol and "near beer" alternatives. These beverages aimed to provide a beer-like experience with significantly reduced alcohol content.

2. The Prohibition of Alcohol Sales

Prohibition in the United States - The 18th Amendment to the U.S. Constitution, which prohibited the manufacture, sale, and transportation of alcoholic beverages, had a devastating impact on the American brewing industry. Many breweries were forced to close their doors, while others turned to producing non-alcoholic products.

Brewery Closures - Thousands of breweries across the United States could not survive the Prohibition era. Those that remained in operation often produced non-alcoholic beverages, like root beer or soda, to stay afloat.

3. The Rise of Speakeasies and Illicit Brewing

The Speakeasy Phenomenon - During Prohibition, illegal bars known as "speakeasies" proliferated across the United States. These hidden establishments served bootlegged alcohol, including beer, to patrons.

Illicit Brewing Operations - Some breweries went underground and produced illicit alcohol, contributing to the rise of organized crime. This period saw the emergence of bootleggers and smuggling networks.

4. Brewing Innovations and Survival

Brewing for Survival - Some breweries adapted to the changing landscape by producing malt extracts, brewing supplies, or non-alcoholic products. This allowed them to remain in business and avoid closure.

The Birth of the Beer Can - The Prohibition era witnessed the introduction of the beer can, which allowed breweries to package non-alcoholic products and adapt to changing consumer preferences.

5. International Responses to Temperance

Temperance in Other Countries - The effects of the Temperance Movement varied from one country to another. Some nations, like Canada, implemented various forms of alcohol regulation, while others, like Ireland, saw the emergence of homebrewing and the "shebeen" culture.

6. The Return of Legal Brewing

The Repeal of Prohibition - The 21st Amendment to the U.S. Constitution in 1933 repealed the 18th Amendment, ending Prohibition. This event marked the return of legal brewing and alcohol sales in the United States.

Challenges for Brewers - The brewing industry faced numerous challenges in reestablishing itself after Prohibition. Many breweries had been out of business for over a decade and needed to rebuild their operations.

7. The Modern Brewing Landscape

Consolidation and Mega-Breweries - The brewing industry underwent significant consolidation in the post-

Prohibition era, leading to the rise of mega-breweries that dominated the market.

Craft Beer Revolution - The late 20th century saw the birth of the craft beer movement, with small, independent breweries focusing on traditional brewing methods and a wide range of beer styles. This movement challenged the dominance of mega-breweries.

Conclusion

The Temperance Movement had a profound and lasting impact on the brewing industry. From the decline of traditional beer styles to the rise of speakeasies, the Prohibition era was a transformative period for brewers. The repeal of Prohibition marked the beginning of a new chapter in brewing history, with the modern craft beer movement providing an alternative to the dominance of mega-breweries. In the following sections, we will explore the Craft Beer Revolution and its influence on the brewing landscape.

Chapter 4: Prohibition in America
The Passage of the 18th Amendment

In this chapter, we delve into the Prohibition era in the United States, a pivotal period marked by the complete ban on the manufacture, sale, and transportation of alcoholic beverages. We begin by examining the passage of the 18th Amendment, a historic legislative milestone that ushered in the era of Prohibition.

The 18th Amendment to the United States Constitution, ratified in 1919, stands as one of the most significant and transformative legislative actions in American history. Its journey from proposal to ratification was a complex and contentious process that reflected the changing social and political landscape of the early 20th century.

Background and Context

Rising Temperance Sentiment - The late 19th and early 20th centuries saw a growing temperance movement in the United States. Concerns about the impact of alcohol on society, coupled with the influence of religious groups and women's organizations, contributed to the momentum for alcohol restrictions.

Pre-Prohibition State Laws - Several states had already implemented various forms of alcohol restrictions before the 18th Amendment. These included local option laws, Sunday sales bans, and dry counties.

The Push for a Federal Amendment

The Role of Advocacy Groups - Organizations such as the Anti-Saloon League (ASL) and the Women's Christian Temperance Union (WCTU) were instrumental in advocating for a federal constitutional amendment to ban alcohol nationwide.

The ASL's Influence - The ASL, under the leadership of Wayne Wheeler, played a particularly crucial role. It used a combination of grassroots organizing, lobbying, and political pressure to gain support for Prohibition.

The Temperance Message - Advocates for the 18th Amendment argued that alcohol was a root cause of societal problems, including poverty, crime, and domestic violence. They believed that Prohibition would lead to a more morally upright and orderly society.

Political Developments

1916 Presidential Election - The 1916 presidential election became a significant turning point for the temperance movement. Both major parties included support for Prohibition in their platforms, reflecting the widespread popularity of the cause.

The Role of the Women's Suffrage Movement

The women's suffrage movement, which secured the right to vote for women in 1920 with the 19th Amendment, aligned itself with the temperance cause. Women's suffrage added a potent political force to the Prohibition movement.

The Legislative Process

Congressional Action

After the 18th Amendment was proposed by Congress, it required ratification by three-fourths of the states. The amendment underwent intense debates and scrutiny during this process.

State Ratification

State-by-state ratification of the 18th Amendment occurred between 1919 and 1933. The process revealed regional variations in support for Prohibition.

Enforcement and Implementation

The Volstead Act

To clarify the 18th Amendment's provisions and outline the specifics of enforcement, the Volstead Act was passed in 1919. This legislation defined what constituted "intoxicating liquors" and established penalties for violations.

Challenges and Resistance

Prohibition faced numerous challenges, including the growth of illegal speakeasies, bootlegging operations, and organized crime involvement in the illicit alcohol trade.

Social and Economic Consequences

The Impact on Society - Prohibition had far-reaching consequences on American society. It changed social habits, led to the rise of underground drinking establishments, and created a culture of secrecy around alcohol.

Economic Effects - The brewing industry, in particular, was severely impacted, with many breweries forced to close, downsize, or shift to producing non-alcoholic beverages.

The Legacy of the 18th Amendment

Repeal and the 21st Amendment - The failures and challenges of Prohibition eventually led to its repeal with the 21st Amendment in 1933. This marked the end of the 18th Amendment and the return to legal alcohol production and sales.

Lessons Learned - The Prohibition era left a lasting legacy, influencing debates over alcohol regulation, individual liberties, and the role of government in personal choices.

Conclusion

The passage of the 18th Amendment was a watershed moment in American history, representing a dramatic shift in the nation's approach to alcohol. Prohibition, with its complex history and multifaceted impact, continues to be studied and debated as a pivotal chapter in the country's social and political evolution. In the following sections, we will explore the Roaring Twenties, the effects of Prohibition on brewing industry workers, and the eventual return of legal brewing.

The Roaring Twenties: Bootlegging and Speakeasies

As we explore the Prohibition era in the United States, it's essential to delve into the vibrant yet clandestine world of the Roaring Twenties. This section explores the rise of bootlegging, the proliferation of speakeasies, and the unique culture that emerged during this tumultuous period.

The Prohibition era of the 1920s gave rise to a dynamic and subversive culture that thrived in the shadows. The Roaring Twenties, marked by unprecedented social change and artistic innovation, was also a time of defiance against the ban on alcohol.

1. The Rise of Bootlegging

Bootlegging Defined - Bootlegging referred to the illegal production, distribution, and sale of alcoholic beverages during Prohibition. Bootleggers operated covert operations, often in hidden locations, to evade law enforcement.

Bootlegging Networks - Elaborate bootlegging networks emerged across the country, with criminal organizations and entrepreneurs capitalizing on the demand for alcohol. These operations ranged from small-scale moonshining to large-scale smuggling.

Famous Bootleggers - Figures like Al Capone in Chicago and George Remus in Cincinnati became infamous for their involvement in bootlegging. They controlled vast empires built on illegal alcohol trade.

Violence and Crime - The competition for control of bootlegging territories often led to violent conflicts, contributing to the rise of organized crime in America.

2. The Proliferation of Speakeasies

Speakeasies Defined - Speakeasies were secret, unlicensed bars or clubs that served alcohol during Prohibition. The name "speakeasy" derived from the need for patrons to speak quietly or "easily" to avoid detection.

Speakeasy Culture - Speakeasies were known for their intimate and underground ambiance. They featured jazz music, dancing, and an air of excitement that contrasted sharply with the temperance era's sobriety.

Famous Speakeasies - Some speakeasies became legendary, such as the Cotton Club in Harlem, the Stork Club in New York City, and the Green Mill in Chicago. These venues attracted both locals and celebrities.

The Role of Women - Speakeasies played a role in changing gender dynamics. Women could patronize these venues freely, often without male escorts, marking a departure from earlier social norms.

3. Cultural Impact

The Jazz Age - The Roaring Twenties coincided with the Jazz Age, and speakeasies played a crucial role in popularizing jazz music. Musicians like Louis Armstrong and Duke Ellington performed in these venues.

Art and Literature - The spirit of rebellion and innovation of the era influenced art, literature, and fashion. The works of writers like F. Scott Fitzgerald and artists like Georgia O'Keeffe captured the essence of the time.

Flappers and Fashion - The flapper culture, characterized by its rejection of traditional norms and embrace of short dresses, bobbed hair, and social independence, became synonymous with the Roaring Twenties.

4. Law Enforcement and Corruption

The Cat-and-Mouse Game - Law enforcement agencies attempted to enforce Prohibition, but the sheer scale of illegal alcohol activities made it a challenging task. Many law enforcement officers were susceptible to corruption.

Prohibition Agents - Prohibition agents, tasked with enforcing alcohol laws, often found themselves facing threats, bribery attempts, and violence from bootleggers and speakeasy operators.

End of an Era

The Great Depression and Public Sentiment - As the Great Depression struck in the early 1930s, public sentiment began to shift. Prohibition was seen as a failed social experiment that had caused economic hardship and fueled crime.

The 21st Amendment - In 1933, the 21st Amendment to the U.S. Constitution was ratified, repealing the 18th Amendment and ending Prohibition. Legal alcohol production and sales returned, marking the end of a turbulent era.

Legacy

Impact on American Culture - The Roaring Twenties and the Prohibition era left an indelible mark on American culture. The era's cultural innovations, from jazz music to flapper fashion, continue to influence art and entertainment today.

Balancing Regulation - The Prohibition era highlighted the challenges of regulating personal choices and the role of government in individuals' lives, sparking ongoing debates about alcohol regulation.

Conclusion

The Roaring Twenties, characterized by bootlegging, speakeasies, and cultural dynamism, was a unique and transformative period in American history. The subversion of Prohibition laws and the emergence of a vibrant underground culture challenged the very notion of a ban on alcohol. In the following sections, we will explore the effects of Prohibition on brewing industry workers, the aftermath of the 21st Amendment, and the enduring legacy of this era.

The Effects of Prohibition on Brewing Industry Workers

In our exploration of the Prohibition era in the United States, it's crucial to understand how this sweeping ban on alcohol had profound and lasting effects on the individuals who worked within the brewing industry. This section delves into the impact of Prohibition on the lives and livelihoods of brewing industry workers.

The brewing industry, once a flourishing and vital part of the American economy, faced unprecedented challenges during the Prohibition era. Brewing industry workers, including brewers, bottlers, delivery drivers, and tavern employees, experienced profound disruptions to their careers and lives.

1. The Brewing Industry Before Prohibition

A Thriving Industry - Prior to Prohibition, the brewing industry in the United States was a major employer, with thousands of breweries across the country. It provided jobs to a diverse workforce, from skilled brewers to manual laborers.

Brewery Workers - The brewing industry employed a wide range of workers, including brewers, maltsters, coopers, cellar workers, bottlers, and quality control personnel. Many of these workers had specialized skills.

Taverns and Saloons - Taverns and saloons served as important venues for socializing and consuming beer. Bartenders, waitstaff, and musicians relied on these establishments for their livelihoods.

2. The Impact of Prohibition

Brewery Closures - Prohibition resulted in the closure of the vast majority of breweries in the United States. Without the legal ability to produce and sell beer, breweries faced bankruptcy or had to pivot to other industries.

Unemployment and Job Loss - The sudden closure of breweries and related businesses led to massive unemployment within the brewing industry. Workers with specialized skills often struggled to find alternative employment.

Economic Hardships - Families dependent on brewery incomes faced economic hardships, and many experienced a significant decline in their standard of living. The loss of brewery jobs had a ripple effect on communities.

3. Adaptation and Survival

Shifts in Employment - Some brewery workers sought employment in other industries, while others transitioned to related roles, such as producing non-alcoholic products or working in the soft drink industry.

Union Activism - Labor unions representing brewery workers played a role in advocating for their members during Prohibition. They lobbied for workers' rights and supported efforts to repeal Prohibition.

4. Speakeasies and Bootlegging

Alternative Employment - Some former brewery workers found employment in the speakeasy and bootlegging industries, where they could use their knowledge of alcohol production and distribution.

Risk and Criminality - Working in illegal alcohol operations was not without risks. Law enforcement crackdowns and gang violence in the illegal alcohol trade made these jobs dangerous.

5. The End of Prohibition and Its Aftermath

The 21st Amendment - The 21st Amendment, ratified in 1933, repealed the 18th Amendment and ended Prohibition. Legal alcohol production and sales returned, leading to the reopening of breweries.

Challenges of Reopening - Reopening breweries posed challenges, as many had been out of operation for over a decade. Infrastructure, equipment, and skilled personnel had to be rebuilt.

Legacy and Continued Employment - The brewing industry, although forever changed by Prohibition, experienced a resurgence after the 21st Amendment. Workers returned to their craft, and new opportunities arose in the evolving beer landscape.

Conclusion

The effects of Prohibition on brewing industry workers were profound and multifaceted. Many experienced unemployment, economic hardship, and the need to adapt to new employment opportunities. The repeal of Prohibition marked a turning point, allowing the brewing industry and its workers to rebuild and contribute to the post-Prohibition resurgence of American brewing. In the following sections, we will explore the aftermath of the 21st Amendment and the enduring legacy of the Prohibition era.

Repeal and the Return of Legal Brewing

As we continue to explore the Prohibition era in the United States, this section delves into the pivotal moment when the 21st Amendment was ratified, repealing the 18th Amendment and ending Prohibition. We'll examine the return of legal brewing and its impact on the brewing industry and society at large.

The repeal of Prohibition in 1933 marked a significant turning point in American history. After over a decade of alcohol bans, the nation experienced a resurgence of legal brewing and the rebirth of a once-thriving industry.

1. The 21st Amendment: Repeal of Prohibition

Ratification of the 21st Amendment - On December 5, 1933, the 21st Amendment to the U.S. Constitution was ratified, officially repealing the 18th Amendment and bringing an end to the nationwide ban on alcohol.

Impact of Repeal - The repeal of Prohibition was met with widespread celebration and relief. It signaled the return to legal alcohol production, sales, and consumption.

2. The Brewing Industry Reawakens

The Reopening of Breweries - Breweries across the country began the process of reopening their doors. Many of these establishments had been closed or repurposed during Prohibition.

Challenges of Rebuilding - The reopening of breweries posed several challenges. Equipment and infrastructure often required extensive repairs or replacement, and skilled personnel needed to be rehired or retrained.

Innovation and Consolidation - Some breweries embraced technological innovations that had emerged during Prohibition, such as advances in refrigeration and packaging. Meanwhile, others sought consolidation to compete in the post-Prohibition market.

3. The Return of Variety

Revival of Traditional Styles - With the return of legal brewing came a resurgence of traditional beer styles, including ales, lagers, stouts, and porters. Breweries revived old recipes and techniques.

Emergence of New Styles - The post-Prohibition era also witnessed the emergence of new beer styles and innovations, including lighter lagers, pilsners, and the beginnings of the American craft beer movement.

4. The Impact on Society

Social and Cultural Shifts - The end of Prohibition had a profound impact on American society. Speakeasies closed, and a culture of secrecy around alcohol consumption gave way to more open and regulated drinking establishments.

The Return of Taverns and Bars - Taverns and bars, once at the heart of American social life, began to reestablish themselves as hubs for socializing and entertainment.

5. Legal Framework and Regulation

The Three-Tier System - In many states, a three-tier system of alcohol distribution was established, consisting of producers, distributors, and retailers. This system aimed to prevent monopolies and ensure the safe and responsible distribution of alcohol.

State-by-State Variation - States had the authority to regulate alcohol within their borders, leading to variations in alcohol laws and regulations across the country.

6. Brewing and the World Wars

World War II and Brewing - During World War II, breweries played a role in supporting the war effort by producing beer for military personnel overseas.

Post-War Brewing - The post-World War II period saw a renewed emphasis on marketing and branding by breweries, as they sought to capture the post-war consumer market.

7. The Birth of the Craft Beer Movement

Precursors to Craft Beer - While large breweries dominated the post-Prohibition landscape, a small number of entrepreneurs and enthusiasts laid the groundwork for the craft beer movement that would emerge later in the 20th century.

The Craft Beer Pioneers - Key figures in the early craft beer movement, such as Fritz Maytag and Jack McAuliffe, began to challenge the dominance of mega-breweries by focusing on traditional brewing methods and unique, high-quality beer.

Conclusion

The repeal of Prohibition marked the return of legal brewing in the United States, ending a period of social and economic upheaval. It ushered in a new era of brewing, with the resurgence of traditional styles and the beginnings of the craft beer movement. In the following sections, we will explore the craft beer revolution, the impact of consolidation on beer variety, and the enduring legacy of this transformative period.

Chapter 5: Brewing Innovations and the Rebirth of Beer

Post-Prohibition Brewing Reforms

In this chapter, we explore the period following the repeal of Prohibition in the United States. With the return of legal brewing, this section focuses on the reforms and changes in the brewing industry as it emerged from the constraints of Prohibition and looked to reestablish itself in American society.

The end of Prohibition in 1933 marked a momentous shift for the brewing industry in the United States. As breweries reopened their doors, they faced both challenges and opportunities that spurred significant reforms.

1. Regulatory Changes

Revised Alcohol Laws - The repeal of Prohibition required the creation of new alcohol regulations and licensing systems. States took different approaches, leading to varying alcohol laws and distribution models.

The Three-Tier System - In many states, a three-tier system was established, consisting of producers, distributors, and retailers. This system aimed to prevent monopolies and maintain control over the distribution and sale of alcohol.

2. Quality Control and Standards

Brewing Technology Advances - The post-Prohibition era saw the introduction of modern brewing equipment and techniques. Brewers began to adopt scientific methods to ensure consistency and quality.

Quality Assurance Programs - Some breweries implemented quality control and assurance programs to maintain high standards for their products. These efforts included testing for flavor consistency and product shelf life.

3. Standardization and Branding

Labeling and Packaging - Breweries began to standardize labeling and packaging to differentiate their products. Labels featured branding, information about alcohol content, and warnings about responsible consumption.

Advertising and Marketing - Breweries invested in advertising and marketing campaigns to promote their brands and products. This led to the emergence of iconic beer advertising, such as the Budweiser Clydesdales.

4. Industry Consolidation

Consolidation Trends - Despite the end of Prohibition, many breweries struggled to survive in the competitive post-Prohibition landscape. Some breweries merged or consolidated to pool resources and reduce costs.

Rise of Mega-Breweries - A few breweries emerged as dominant players in the industry, leading to the rise of mega-breweries that produced popular, nationally recognized brands.

5. The Birth of the Beer Can

Invention and Adoption - The beer can, introduced in the post-Prohibition era, revolutionized beer packaging. Canned beer offered convenience, portability, and protection from light and air.

Impact on Industry - The beer can had a profound impact on the brewing industry, as breweries adopted this innovation for mass production and distribution.

6. The Role of Prohibition Survivors

Breweries That Survived Prohibition - Some breweries managed to survive Prohibition through the production of non-alcoholic products, such as soda, ice cream, or malt extract. These businesses transitioned back to brewing beer.

Resilience and Adaptation - Prohibition survivors showcased resilience and adaptability as they reentered the brewing industry, often relying on their pre-Prohibition expertise.

7. Post-War Brewing Landscape

World War II and Brewing - During World War II, breweries played a role in supporting the war effort by producing beer for military personnel overseas.

Consumer Preferences - After World War II, consumer preferences shifted toward lighter lagers, which led to the dominance of brands like Budweiser, Coors, and Miller.

Conclusion

The period following the repeal of Prohibition witnessed significant reforms in the brewing industry. Regulatory changes, quality control measures, standardization, and branding all contributed to the industry's recovery and growth. The emergence of mega-breweries and the introduction of the beer can were notable developments that shaped the brewing landscape. In the following sections, we will explore the resurgence of small breweries, advances in brewing technology, and the birth of the craft beer movement, which would bring further innovation and diversity to the world of beer.

The Return of Small Breweries

In this chapter, we continue our exploration of the post-Prohibition era in the United States, focusing on the resurgence of small breweries. After the repeal of Prohibition in 1933, the brewing landscape began to shift, with a renewed interest in smaller, independent breweries and a return to traditional brewing methods.

The Return of Small Breweries

The post-Prohibition period saw the emergence of small breweries as a significant force in the American brewing industry. This section delves into the revival of small-scale brewing operations and their impact on the beer landscape.

1. The Pioneers of Small Brewing

Early Visionaries - In the years following Prohibition, a few visionary individuals recognized the potential for small-scale, artisanal brewing. They sought to challenge the dominance of mega-breweries.

Fritz Maytag and Anchor Brewing - Fritz Maytag's acquisition of Anchor Brewing Company in 1965 marked a turning point. He became a pioneer of the craft beer movement, reviving traditional brewing methods and saving a historic brewery.

Jack McAuliffe and New Albion - Jack McAuliffe is often credited with opening the first modern microbrewery, New Albion Brewing Company, in 1976. His venture inspired a new generation of brewers.

2. The Microbrewery Movement

Rise of the Microbrewery - The microbrewery movement gained momentum in the late 20th century. Microbreweries were characterized by their small-scale production, focus on quality, and commitment to unique flavors.

The Brewing Renaissance - Microbreweries played a crucial role in rekindling interest in diverse beer styles and brewing traditions. They reintroduced consumers to a wide range of beer options.

3. Advances in Brewing Technology

Innovations in Small Brewing - Small breweries embraced technological innovations that allowed them to maintain consistency and quality in their products. This included temperature control, fermentation science, and equipment improvements.

Quality and Consistency - The focus on quality became a hallmark of small breweries. Brewers prioritized the use of fresh ingredients and precise brewing techniques.

4. The Craft Beer Boom

Craft Beer Defined - The term "craft beer" came to define small breweries that emphasized traditional methods, independence, and a commitment to producing distinctive, high-quality beer.

Craft Beer's Growth - The craft beer movement experienced exponential growth in the late 20th and early 21st centuries. Small breweries expanded across the country, offering a wide array of beer styles.

5. The Impact on Beer Culture

Diverse Beer Styles - The resurgence of small breweries led to a revival of diverse beer styles, including ales, stouts, porters, and Belgian-style beers. Consumers embraced the opportunity to explore new flavors.

Brewpubs and Taprooms - Many small breweries established brewpubs and taprooms, creating spaces where patrons could enjoy fresh, locally brewed beer and engage with the brewing process.

6. Challenges and Sustainability

Market Competition - As the craft beer movement grew, small breweries faced increasing competition from one another and from larger beer producers.

Sustainability and Local Sourcing - Many craft breweries adopted sustainable practices and emphasized local sourcing of ingredients, connecting with environmentally conscious consumers.

7. The Craft Beer Legacy

Influence on Brewing Culture - The craft beer movement has left an enduring legacy, influencing brewing culture and consumer preferences. It has sparked creativity, experimentation, and a renewed appreciation for beer as a craft.

Economic Impact - Craft breweries have contributed significantly to local economies, job creation, and tourism, making them important players in regional development.

Conclusion

The resurgence of small breweries in the post-Prohibition era transformed the American brewing landscape. Visionaries like Fritz Maytag and Jack McAuliffe paved the way for the craft beer movement, which continues to thrive today. The commitment to quality, innovation, and tradition in craft brewing has had a profound and lasting impact on beer culture and the brewing industry as a whole. In the following sections, we will further explore advances in brewing technology and the enduring legacy of the craft beer movement.

Advances in Brewing Technology

In this chapter, we continue our exploration of the post-Prohibition era in the United States, focusing on the advances in brewing technology that transformed the brewing industry. As small breweries emerged and the craft beer movement gained momentum, brewing technology played a pivotal role in ensuring consistency, quality, and innovation in beer production.

The post-Prohibition period witnessed significant innovations in brewing technology, from equipment improvements to fermentation science. These advances reshaped the brewing landscape and paved the way for the modern craft beer movement.

1. Temperature Control

Fermentation Temperature Management - Controlling fermentation temperatures became a critical aspect of brewing. Brewers adopted temperature-controlled fermentation vessels to ensure consistency in flavor profiles.

Yeast Management - Maintaining optimal fermentation temperatures allowed brewers to manage yeast performance and produce clean and desirable beer styles.

2. Quality Control and Assurance

Laboratory Techniques - Small breweries began to incorporate laboratory techniques to analyze and monitor the quality of ingredients, wort, and finished beer. This ensured the absence of contaminants and consistent product quality.

Sensory Evaluation - Brewers and quality control experts developed sensory evaluation methods to assess flavor, aroma, and overall beer quality. This allowed for fine-tuning of recipes and processes.

3. Equipment Innovations

Modern Brewhouses - Breweries invested in modern brewhouse equipment, including mash tuns, lauter tuns, and kettles, designed to improve efficiency and consistency in the brewing process.

Kegs and Packaging - Innovations in kegs and packaging materials, such as kegging machines and canning lines, improved the handling and distribution of beer, ensuring freshness and quality.

4. Ingredient Selection and Processing

Hop Innovations - The craft beer movement rekindled interest in hop varieties and flavors. Advances in hop processing and preservation allowed brewers to experiment with unique hop profiles.

Malt Varieties - Small breweries explored a broader range of malt varieties, including specialty and roasted malts, to craft distinctive beer styles.

5. Automation and Control Systems

Brewery Automation - Some breweries implemented automation and control systems to monitor and manage various aspects of the brewing process, from mashing to fermentation.

Data-Driven Brewing - Brewers used data collection and analysis to make informed decisions about recipe adjustments and process optimization.

6. Yeast Management and Strain Development

Yeast Culturing - Small breweries invested in yeast propagation and culturing techniques to maintain yeast health and consistency.

Yeast Strain Development - The craft beer movement led to the development of new yeast strains with unique flavor profiles, allowing for greater experimentation in brewing.

7. Sustainability in Brewing

Energy Efficiency - Breweries adopted energy-efficient practices, including heat recovery systems and solar power, to reduce their environmental footprint.

Water Conservation - Water management and conservation became a priority, with breweries implementing water recycling and purification systems.

8. Collaborative Research and Knowledge Sharing

Brewing Associations - Brewing associations and organizations facilitated knowledge sharing and collaborative research among brewers, fostering innovation.

Educational Programs - The growth of brewing programs and institutions dedicated to brewing education helped disseminate brewing knowledge and best practices.

Conclusion

Advances in brewing technology played a central role in the transformation of the brewing industry in the post-Prohibition era. Temperature control, quality assurance, equipment improvements, and ingredient innovation elevated the quality and diversity of beer styles. Automation and data-driven brewing brought precision to the brewing process, while sustainability efforts underscored a commitment to responsible brewing practices. These technological advancements, coupled with the passion and creativity of brewers, laid the foundation for the craft beer movement's continued growth and innovation. In the following sections, we will delve deeper into the enduring legacy of this movement and its impact on the brewing landscape.

The Birth of the Beer Can and Bottling Innovations

In this chapter, we explore the period following the repeal of Prohibition in the United States, focusing on the technological innovations that reshaped the brewing industry. This section delves into the birth of the beer can and other bottling innovations, revolutionizing how beer was packaged and distributed.

The post-Prohibition era brought about significant changes in how beer was packaged and delivered to consumers. The introduction of the beer can and other bottling innovations transformed the industry and contributed to its growth.

1. The Emergence of the Beer Can

The Advent of Canned Beer - The concept of beer in cans was initially met with skepticism. However, in the early 1930s, brewers and can manufacturers began experimenting with the idea.

Early Beer Can Designs - The first beer cans featured flat tops that required a church-key opener. These early designs had limitations but demonstrated the potential for canned beer.

The Pull-Tab Revolution - In the 1960s, the invention of the pull-tab, or ring-pull, changed the game. It made opening canned beer much easier and more convenient for consumers.

2. Benefits of Canned Beer

Preservation of Freshness - Cans offered superior protection from light and oxygen, ensuring beer freshness and preventing off-flavors.

Portability and Convenience - Cans were lightweight, easy to transport, and less prone to breakage, making them ideal for outdoor activities and events.

Sustainability - Aluminum cans were recyclable, and breweries promoted the environmental benefits of canned packaging.

3. Bottling Innovations

Return to Glass Bottles - Glass bottles made a comeback in the post-Prohibition era, with innovations in bottle design and sealing methods.

The Long Neck Bottle - The introduction of the long neck bottle, similar to the modern beer bottle, became an industry standard.

Crown Caps and Sealing Technology - Advances in crown cap technology improved the sealing and preservation of bottled beer.

4. Labeling and Branding

Label Design and Brand Identity - Breweries focused on label design to differentiate their products on store shelves. Labels became an important part of brand identity and marketing.

Information and Warnings - Labels included information about alcohol content, government warnings, and responsible consumption messages.

5. Packaging Materials

Cardboard Packaging - Cardboard packaging, including six-pack carriers, became popular for cans and bottles, providing convenient and eco-friendly options for consumers.

Packaging Innovations - Breweries experimented with packaging innovations, such as the "sixer," which held six bottles or cans securely.

6. Distribution and Market Expansion

Wider Distribution - The introduction of canned beer and improved packaging allowed breweries to expand their reach to regions previously inaccessible.

Impact on Brewery Size - Smaller breweries benefited from the ability to distribute their products more widely, contributing to the growth of craft brewing.

7. Challenges and Controversies

Consumer Acceptance - Initially, consumers were skeptical about the quality of canned beer, but over time, perception changed.

Environmental Concerns - The environmental impact of aluminum cans and glass bottles raised concerns, leading to efforts to minimize the industry's footprint.

8. Modern Packaging Innovations

Craft Beer and Artistic Labeling - Craft breweries embraced artistic label design as a means of expressing their unique brand identities.

Innovations in Packaging Sizes - Craft breweries often offered a variety of packaging sizes, including 16-ounce cans and large-format bottles, catering to diverse consumer preferences.

Conclusion

The birth of the beer can and other bottling innovations revolutionized the packaging and distribution of beer in the post-Prohibition era. Cans offered practicality, convenience, and preservation of freshness, while glass bottles underwent refinements in design and sealing technology. These innovations expanded the market reach of breweries and contributed to the growth of the brewing industry. In the following sections, we will further explore the impact of consolidation on beer variety and the enduring legacy of the craft beer movement.

Chapter 6: Consolidation and the Rise of Beer Giants

The Growth of Mega-Breweries

In this chapter, we delve into the era of consolidation within the brewing industry, marked by the growth of mega-breweries. As the post-Prohibition landscape evolved, a handful of breweries emerged as dominant players, fundamentally altering the brewing industry's structure and dynamics.

The post-Prohibition period witnessed the rise of mega-breweries, large-scale brewing corporations that came to dominate the American beer market. This section explores the factors that fueled their growth and the impact they had on the brewing landscape.

1. Brewing Industry Consolidation

Market Forces - The brewing industry in the United States underwent significant consolidation in the mid-20th century. Several factors contributed to this trend, including changes in consumer preferences, economies of scale, and the pursuit of national and international markets.

2. The Emergence of Mega-Breweries

Industry Leaders - A small number of breweries emerged as industry leaders, dominating both domestic and global markets. Names like Anheuser-Busch, Miller Brewing

Company, and Coors Brewing Company became synonymous with American beer.

Economies of Scale - Mega-breweries leveraged economies of scale to produce beer more efficiently and at lower costs. This allowed them to offer competitive prices and maintain high-profit margins.

3. Branding and Marketing Strategies

National and International Expansion - Mega-breweries pursued aggressive expansion strategies, entering new markets both domestically and internationally. Their brands became household names worldwide.

Advertising Campaigns - Mega-breweries invested heavily in advertising campaigns, creating iconic and memorable marketing efforts to promote their products.

4. Acquisition and Consolidation

Brewery Acquisitions - Mega-breweries acquired smaller breweries and regional competitors, incorporating their brands and production facilities into their portfolios.

Brand Consolidation - The consolidation of brands led to a narrowing of beer options in some markets, with mega-breweries focusing on a smaller number of flagship products.

5. Standardization and Streamlining

Consistency and Uniformity - Mega-breweries prioritized consistency in product quality and flavor profiles, ensuring that consumers could expect the same taste from their brands nationwide.

Streamlining Production - The production process was streamlined to reduce costs and increase efficiency. This often involved centralizing production at a few large facilities.

6. Impact on Beer Variety

Diversity vs. Homogenization - The rise of mega-breweries had both positive and negative effects on beer variety. While they introduced consumers to a few iconic styles, it also led to a certain level of homogenization in the market.

Craft Beer Reaction - The dominance of mega-breweries contributed to the rise of the craft beer movement, as consumers sought more diverse and unique beer options.

7. Challenges and Controversies

Antitrust Concerns - The consolidation of the brewing industry raised antitrust concerns, as it limited competition and reduced consumer choice in some markets.

Quality vs. Quantity - Critics argued that mega-breweries prioritized quantity over quality, leading to perceptions of lower-quality beer.

8. The Globalization of Mega-Breweries

International Expansion - Mega-breweries extended their reach to international markets, often acquiring foreign breweries and integrating them into their global operations.

Global Beer Brands - Brands owned by mega-breweries became global beer brands, available in countries around the world.

Conclusion

The growth of mega-breweries marked a significant shift in the brewing industry, with a small number of corporations dominating the market. Their strategies, including economies of scale, aggressive marketing, and brand consolidation, reshaped the American beer landscape. However, their dominance also spurred reactions within the industry, leading to the emergence of the craft beer movement, which we will explore in the following sections.

Beer Marketing and Branding Strategies

In this chapter, we delve into the era of consolidation within the brewing industry, marked by the growth of mega-breweries. As the post-Prohibition landscape evolved, a handful of breweries emerged as dominant players, fundamentally altering the brewing industry's structure and dynamics.

One of the key elements of the success of mega-breweries was their mastery of marketing and branding. This section explores the innovative strategies they employed to establish and promote their beer brands.

1. Building Iconic Brands

Brand Identity - Mega-breweries recognized the importance of creating strong and memorable brand identities. They invested in logos, slogans, and packaging designs that resonated with consumers.

Iconic Logos - Logos like the Budweiser Clydesdales, the Coors Mountains, and the Miller High Life Girl in the Moon became synonymous with their respective brands and left a lasting impression.

2. Advertising Campaigns

Television Advertising - The rise of television as a medium for advertising allowed mega-breweries to reach a mass audience. They crafted memorable commercials that often featured humor, emotion, or patriotism.

Super Bowl Commercials - Mega-breweries became known for their Super Bowl commercials, often creating the most anticipated and talked-about ads during the big game.

3. Sponsorships and Events

Sports Sponsorships - Mega-breweries sponsored major sporting events, teams, and athletes. This not only provided visibility but also associated their brands with the excitement of sports.

Music and Entertainment - They also sponsored concerts, music festivals, and other entertainment events, aligning their brands with popular culture.

4. Targeting Specific Demographics

Demographic Marketing - Mega-breweries used demographic data to target specific consumer groups. They developed advertising campaigns tailored to different age groups, genders, and lifestyles.

Appealing to Young Adults - Strategies to attract young adult consumers often included ads featuring youthful and adventurous themes.

5. Packaging Innovations

Cans vs. Bottles - Mega-breweries used packaging as a way to differentiate their products. They highlighted the convenience and freshness preservation of cans or the premium image of bottles.

Limited-Edition Packaging - Special packaging releases, such as holiday-themed labels or collector's cans, created buzz and encouraged sales.

6. Responsible Consumption Messages

Promoting Responsibility - As concerns about alcohol consumption and its consequences grew, mega-breweries launched campaigns promoting responsible drinking and discouraging drunk driving.

Alcohol Content and Calorie Information - Labels started including information about alcohol by volume (ABV) and calorie content to inform consumers.

7. Expanding Global Reach

International Marketing - Mega-breweries expanded their marketing efforts to target global audiences. They adapted their campaigns to suit the cultural nuances of different countries.

Acquisitions and Local Brands - Acquiring local breweries allowed mega-breweries to maintain a presence in specific regions and market their brands as "local."

8. Challenges and Controversies

Critiques of Manipulative Marketing - Critics accused mega-breweries of using manipulative tactics to influence consumer choices, such as subliminal messaging or appealing to societal norms.

Response from Craft Brewers - The craft beer movement, in response to these marketing strategies, emphasized transparency, authenticity, and a rejection of mass-produced beer.

Conclusion

Mega-breweries' marketing and branding strategies played a pivotal role in their ascent to dominance in the brewing industry. They successfully created iconic brands, crafted memorable advertising campaigns, and targeted specific demographics. These strategies allowed them to not only establish a stronghold on the American beer market but also expand their influence globally. In the following sections, we will explore the craft beer revolution, which emerged as a reaction to the marketing and brewing practices of the beer giants.

The Battle for Market Dominance

In this chapter, we delve into the era of consolidation within the brewing industry, marked by the growth of mega-breweries. As the post-Prohibition landscape evolved, a handful of breweries emerged as dominant players, fundamentally altering the brewing industry's structure and dynamics.

The rise of mega-breweries ushered in an era of intense competition for market dominance. This section explores the strategies employed by these brewing giants to secure their positions and maintain their dominance in the American beer market.

1. Expanding Product Portfolios

Brand Diversification - Mega-breweries expanded their product portfolios by introducing a range of beer brands, each targeting different market segments and consumer preferences.

Acquisitions of Regional Breweries - They acquired regional and smaller breweries, allowing them to tap into the popularity of local and craft-style beers.

2. Price Wars and Competitive Pricing

Economies of Scale - Mega-breweries leveraged their size to produce beer at lower costs, enabling them to offer competitive pricing to consumers.

Price Promotions - They engaged in price wars and offered promotions to gain a competitive edge in retail and on-premises establishments.

3. Distribution Networks

National Distribution - Mega-breweries established extensive distribution networks, ensuring that their products were available in convenience stores, supermarkets, bars, and restaurants across the country.

Tied-House Practices - Some breweries used tied-house practices, owning or controlling bars and retail outlets to exclusively feature their products.

4. Marketing and Advertising Strategies

Mass Media Campaigns - They continued to invest heavily in mass media advertising, ensuring that their brands remained top-of-mind for consumers.

Sponsorship Deals - Mega-breweries secured sponsorship deals with sports leagues, music festivals, and cultural events to maintain visibility and attract a wide audience.

5. Global Expansion

International Markets - Mega-breweries pursued international expansion, exporting their brands to countries around the world and acquiring foreign breweries.

Local Adaptations - They adapted their marketing and product offerings to suit the tastes and cultural nuances of different international markets.

6. Lobbying and Political Influence

Industry Lobbying - Mega-breweries engaged in lobbying efforts to influence alcohol regulations and taxation, sometimes to the detriment of smaller competitors.

Community Engagement - They often presented themselves as responsible corporate citizens, investing in community initiatives and philanthropic efforts to gain public support.

7. Craft Brewery Acquisition Strategies

Purchasing Craft Breweries - Recognizing the popularity of craft beer, mega-breweries acquired craft breweries while allowing them a degree of autonomy.

Craft Branding and Marketing - They preserved the craft branding and marketing of the acquired breweries to tap into the growing craft beer movement.

8. Challenges and Controversies

Antitrust Concerns - The consolidation of mega-breweries raised antitrust concerns, as their dominance limited competition and consumer choice.

Consumer Perception - Critics argued that the strategies employed by mega-breweries, including price wars and acquisitions, stifled innovation and diversity in the beer market.

Conclusion

The battle for market dominance in the brewing industry led to intense competition among mega-breweries. They utilized diverse strategies, from brand diversification and pricing wars to distribution networks and global expansion, to secure their positions. However, their dominance also spurred reactions within the industry, such as the craft beer movement, which sought to challenge their market share. In the following sections, we will explore the craft beer revolution and its impact on the brewing landscape.

The Impact of Consolidation on Beer Variety

In this chapter, we delve into the era of consolidation within the brewing industry, marked by the growth of mega-breweries. As the post-Prohibition landscape evolved, a handful of breweries emerged as dominant players, fundamentally altering the brewing industry's structure and dynamics.

The rise of mega-breweries and the consolidation of the brewing industry had profound effects on the variety of beer available to consumers. This section explores how the dominance of beer giants influenced the diversity of beer styles and flavors.

1. The Homogenization of Beer

Standardization - Mega-breweries, in their pursuit of efficiency and consistency, often standardized their beer recipes, resulting in a narrower range of flavor profiles.

Emphasis on Mass Appeal - To maximize market share, beer giants focused on producing beer styles that appealed to the broadest possible consumer base. This led to a prevalence of lighter, milder lagers.

2. Decline of Regional and Local Styles

Regional Specialties - Before consolidation, many regions had their unique beer styles and traditions. The dominance of mega-breweries often resulted in the decline or disappearance of these regional specialties.

Closure of Local Breweries - The acquisition of smaller regional breweries often led to their closure or the discontinuation of their unique beer offerings.

3. Limited Innovation

Resource Allocation - Mega-breweries allocated significant resources to marketing and distribution, leaving fewer resources for experimentation and innovation in brewing.

Innovation vs. Tradition - The emphasis on brewing beer styles with mass appeal sometimes clashed with traditional brewing methods and unique, innovative recipes.

4. Influence on Craft Beer Movement

Craft Beer as a Reaction - The craft beer movement emerged in response to the perceived homogenization of beer and the desire for more diverse and unique options.

Diversity and Experimentation - Craft breweries sought to fill the void left by the beer giants by producing a wide range of beer styles and embracing experimentation.

5. Limited Shelf Space

Retail and Bar Choices - The dominance of mega-breweries in the market often resulted in limited shelf space for smaller, independent breweries in retail stores and limited tap choices in bars and restaurants.

Craft Beer Advocacy - Craft beer enthusiasts and organizations advocated for greater access to shelf space and tap lines, promoting diversity in beer offerings.

6. Consumer Demand for Variety

Changing Consumer Preferences - Consumer preferences shifted towards more diverse and unique beer options, driven by curiosity and a desire for new flavor experiences.

Craft Beer's Rise in Popularity - The craft beer movement's success was rooted in its ability to offer variety and cater to evolving consumer tastes.

7. Efforts to Maintain Diversity

Craft Brands Owned by Mega-Breweries - Some mega-breweries acquired craft breweries while allowing them a degree of autonomy. This preserved diversity in their portfolios.

Response to Craft Beer Movement - As the craft beer movement gained momentum, some mega-breweries introduced their own craft-style brands to compete in this segment.

8. The Role of Microbreweries

Microbreweries and Brewpubs - Microbreweries and brewpubs played a significant role in maintaining and expanding beer diversity, often experimenting with new styles and flavors.

Local Impact - They connected with local communities and offered unique, small-batch brews that catered to regional tastes.

Conclusion

The consolidation of the brewing industry had a significant impact on beer variety, often leading to the homogenization of beer styles and a decline in regional specialties. However, it also sparked a reaction in the form of the craft beer movement, which sought to reintroduce diversity, innovation, and unique flavors to the market. The battle between beer giants and craft breweries continues to shape the modern brewing landscape, emphasizing the importance of choice and variety for consumers. In the following sections, we will explore the craft beer revolution and its enduring influence on the brewing industry.

Chapter 7: The Craft Beer Revolution

The Birth of the Homebrewing Movement

In this chapter, we delve into the craft beer revolution, a movement that transformed the brewing industry by championing small-scale, independent breweries and a return to traditional brewing methods. This section explores the birth of the homebrewing movement, a foundational element of the craft beer renaissance.

The craft beer revolution was ignited by passionate individuals who sought to break away from the dominance of mega-breweries and reintroduce diversity and innovation into brewing. The homebrewing movement played a pivotal role in this transformation, inspiring a new generation of brewers and beer enthusiasts.

1. Early Homebrewing Pioneers

Charlie Papazian and The Joy of Homebrewing - Charlie Papazian's seminal book, "The Complete Joy of Homebrewing," published in 1984, became a bible for aspiring homebrewers. His accessible and encouraging approach demystified the brewing process.

Homebrewing Associations - Homebrewing associations, such as the American Homebrewers Association (AHA), provided a platform for enthusiasts to connect, share knowledge, and advocate for brewing rights.

2. Legalization of Homebrewing

Prohibition Era Legacy - Homebrewing remained illegal in the United States until 1978 when President Jimmy Carter signed legislation legalizing homebrewing for personal and household use.

Impact of Legalization - The legalization of homebrewing encouraged enthusiasts to experiment and develop their brewing skills openly.

3. The DIY Spirit

Homebuilt Equipment - Homebrewers often built their equipment or adapted household items for brewing, embodying the do-it-yourself (DIY) ethos.

Recipe Development - Experimentation with ingredients and brewing techniques allowed homebrewers to create unique beer recipes and styles.

4. Community and Knowledge Sharing

Homebrew Clubs - Homebrew clubs formed across the country, fostering a sense of community among brewers and providing opportunities to share knowledge and sample each other's creations.

Educational Resources - Homebrewing literature, workshops, and classes proliferated, equipping aspiring brewers with the knowledge and skills needed to craft exceptional beer.

5. Advancements in Homebrewing Technology

Equipment Innovation - The availability of specialized homebrewing equipment and ingredients expanded, making it easier for homebrewers to craft high-quality beer.

Online Resources - The rise of the internet facilitated knowledge sharing and the exchange of brewing tips and techniques among a global community of homebrewers.

6. Homebrewing Competitions

Homebrew Competitions - Amateur brewing competitions emerged, providing homebrewers with opportunities to showcase their creations and receive feedback from experienced judges.

Winning Homebrewers - Some award-winning homebrewers eventually turned their passion into a profession by opening their own craft breweries.

7. Influence on the Craft Beer Movement

Brewers Turned Entrepreneurs - Many early craft brewers had their roots in homebrewing, transitioning from hobbyist to professional brewers.

Diversity of Styles - The experimentation and innovation of homebrewers inspired a diverse array of beer styles within the craft beer movement.

8. The Legalization of Craft Brewing

Pioneering Legislation - As the craft beer movement gained momentum, changes in legislation at the state and federal levels paved the way for small, independent breweries to thrive.

Craft Brewing's Economic Impact - The craft beer industry's economic impact, including job creation and tourism, prompted further support and recognition.

Conclusion

The homebrewing movement played a foundational role in the craft beer revolution, inspiring a new generation of brewers and fostering a culture of experimentation, knowledge sharing, and community. As homebrewers honed their skills and turned their passion into professions, they helped reshape the brewing landscape, challenging the dominance of mega-breweries and reinvigorating the beer industry with diversity and innovation. In the following sections, we will explore the growth of microbreweries and brewpubs as key elements of the craft beer movement.

Microbreweries and Brewpubs

In this chapter, we delve into the craft beer revolution, a movement that transformed the brewing industry by championing small-scale, independent breweries and a return to traditional brewing methods. This section explores the rise of microbreweries and brewpubs as key elements of the craft beer movement.

As the craft beer movement gained momentum, microbreweries and brewpubs emerged as important players in reshaping the brewing landscape. These small, independent breweries embraced creativity, diversity, and a close connection to their local communities, contributing significantly to the craft beer renaissance.

1. Rise of Microbreweries

Defining Microbreweries - Microbreweries are small-scale breweries that produce limited quantities of beer, typically focusing on quality, flavor, and innovation.

Pioneering Microbreweries - Early microbreweries like Anchor Brewing Company and Sierra Nevada Brewing Company paved the way for the modern craft beer industry.

2. Characteristics of Microbreweries

Small Batches - Microbreweries prioritize small-batch brewing, allowing for experimentation and the production of unique beer styles.

Local Focus - Many microbreweries have a strong local focus, often sourcing ingredients locally and engaging with their communities.

3. Brewpubs: Combining Brewing and Hospitality

Defining Brewpubs - Brewpubs are hybrid establishments that combine a brewery with a restaurant or pub, providing a space for patrons to enjoy beer on-site and often offering food pairings.

Brewpub Origins - The concept of brewpubs has historical roots, but they saw a resurgence in the craft beer movement.

4. Advantages and Challenges

Flexibility and Creativity - Microbreweries and brewpubs have the flexibility to experiment with ingredients, brewing techniques, and beer styles.

Challenges of Scale - Limited production capacity can make it challenging for microbreweries to meet high demand, leading to occasional shortages of popular beers.

5. Craft Brewing Culture

Community Engagement - Microbreweries and brewpubs often engage with their local communities through events, partnerships, and charitable initiatives.

Brewer-Patron Interaction - Patrons can often interact with brewers, fostering a sense of connection and transparency.

6. Impact on the Craft Beer Movement

Diversity and Innovation - Microbreweries and brewpubs have been at the forefront of brewing innovation, introducing new styles and pushing the boundaries of what beer can be.

Craft Beer Tourism - The presence of microbreweries and brewpubs has attracted craft beer enthusiasts and tourists, contributing to local economies.

7. Challenges and Opportunities

Competition and Saturation - The growing number of microbreweries and brewpubs has led to increased competition, requiring breweries to differentiate themselves.

Distribution Challenges - Expanding distribution beyond the local market can be a challenge for microbreweries due to limited production capacity.

8. The Craft Beer Renaissance Continues

Craft Beer's Continued Growth - The craft beer movement continues to evolve, with microbreweries and brewpubs playing a vital role in its growth and diversification.

Influence on Beer Culture - The impact of microbreweries and brewpubs extends beyond brewing, influencing beer culture, and the way consumers think about and appreciate beer.

Conclusion

Microbreweries and brewpubs have been instrumental in the craft beer movement, embodying its spirit of creativity, diversity, and community engagement. Their focus on quality, local sourcing, and experimentation has enriched the beer landscape, offering consumers a wide array of unique and flavorful options. As we explore further, we will delve into the challenges and opportunities faced by these small, independent breweries in a competitive and dynamic industry.

The Pioneers of Craft Beer

In this chapter, we delve into the craft beer revolution, a movement that transformed the brewing industry by championing small-scale, independent breweries and a return to traditional brewing methods. This section explores the pioneers of craft beer, the visionaries and early entrepreneurs who laid the foundation for the craft beer renaissance.

The craft beer movement owes much of its success to the dedication, innovation, and entrepreneurial spirit of its pioneers. These individuals and breweries not only challenged the status quo but also inspired a generation of craft brewers.

1. Fritz Maytag and Anchor Brewing Company

Early Craft Brewer - Fritz Maytag's acquisition of Anchor Brewing Company in 1965 marked a turning point in the craft beer movement. He is often referred to as the "father of modern craft beer."

Reviving Tradition - Maytag focused on reviving traditional brewing methods and recipes, producing iconic beers like Anchor Steam.

2. Ken Grossman and Sierra Nevada Brewing Company

Sierra Nevada's Origins - Ken Grossman founded Sierra Nevada Brewing Company in 1980. The brewery quickly gained recognition for its commitment to quality and innovation.

Pale Ale Revolution - Sierra Nevada's Pale Ale played a crucial role in popularizing hop-forward American Pale Ales.

3. Jim Koch and The Boston Beer Company

Samuel Adams - Jim Koch founded The Boston Beer Company in 1984, with the goal of reintroducing flavorful and traditional beer styles to American consumers.

Craft Beer Revolution Icon - Samuel Adams Boston Lager became an iconic beer of the craft beer movement.

4. Charlie Papazian and Homebrewing Advocacy

Homebrewing Advocate - Charlie Papazian, author of "The Complete Joy of Homebrewing," played a vital role in popularizing homebrewing and educating aspiring brewers.

American Homebrewers Association - Papazian was a co-founder of the American Homebrewers Association, fostering a sense of community among homebrewers.

5. Jack McAuliffe and New Albion Brewing Company

New Albion's Significance - Jack McAuliffe founded New Albion Brewing Company in 1976, one of the first microbreweries in the United States.

Limited Success - Although short-lived, New Albion inspired other brewers to pursue their passion and establish their own craft breweries.

6. Anchor Brewing, Sierra Nevada, and The Boston Beer Company

Craft Beer Success Stories - Anchor Brewing Company, Sierra Nevada Brewing Company, and The Boston Beer Company (Samuel Adams) became successful, enduring icons of the craft beer movement.

Quality and Consistency - These breweries prioritized quality, consistency, and adherence to traditional brewing methods.

7. The Role of Regional Breweries

Reinventing Regional Brewers - Some regional breweries, like New Belgium Brewing Company and Bell's Brewery, embraced craft beer principles and played essential roles in the movement.

Regional Specialties - They often celebrated and showcased regional beer styles and flavors.

8. Craft Beer's Influence on the Brewing Landscape

Craft Beer's Cultural Impact - The success of craft breweries reshaped American beer culture, emphasizing the value of flavor, diversity, and tradition.

Influence on Mega-Breweries - The craft beer movement's success prompted mega-breweries to adapt and introduce craft-style brands to their portfolios.

Conclusion

The pioneers of craft beer laid the foundation for a movement that challenged the dominance of mega-breweries, reintroduced traditional brewing methods, and celebrated flavor and diversity. Their dedication to quality and innovation inspired countless others to enter the world of craft brewing. As we explore further, we will delve into the craft beer revolution's impact on the brewing industry and its enduring legacy in the world of beer.

Craft Beer's Impact on the Brewing Landscape

In this chapter, we delve into the craft beer revolution, a movement that transformed the brewing industry by championing small-scale, independent breweries and a return to traditional brewing methods. This section explores the impact of craft beer on the brewing landscape, both in terms of brewing culture and the industry as a whole.

The craft beer movement not only redefined consumer preferences but also influenced the brewing industry in profound ways. This section explores how craft beer has shaped the brewing landscape.

1. Diverse Beer Styles and Innovation

Expanding the Palette - Craft breweries have introduced an unprecedented variety of beer styles, from IPAs and stouts to sours and barrel-aged beers.

Brewing Innovation - Craft brewers have continually pushed the boundaries of what's possible in brewing, experimenting with ingredients and techniques.

2. Quality and Flavor Focus

Elevating Beer Quality - The craft beer movement prioritized quality and flavor, emphasizing the use of premium ingredients and traditional brewing methods.

Consumer Education - Craft brewers have played a role in educating consumers about the nuances of beer flavors and styles.

3. Local and Independent Brewing

Embracing Localism - The craft beer movement has celebrated local ingredients and flavors, contributing to the resurgence of regional beer styles.

Supporting Independent Brewers - Consumers actively support independent craft breweries, fostering a sense of community and loyalty.

4. Beer Tourism and Brewpub Culture

Destination Breweries - Craft breweries have become destinations for tourists, contributing to the growth of beer tourism in regions like the Pacific Northwest and Colorado.

Brewpub Culture - Brewpubs offer a unique experience by combining brewery operations with hospitality, enhancing consumer engagement.

5. Craft Beer's Economic Impact

Job Creation - The craft beer industry has created jobs in brewing, distribution, retail, and hospitality.

Local Economies - Craft breweries have contributed to the economic development of neighborhoods, towns, and cities, attracting visitors and revenue.

6. Influence on Beer Packaging and Distribution

Canned Craft Beer - The craft beer movement popularized canned beer, emphasizing its benefits for preserving beer quality and portability.

Distribution Challenges - Craft brewers have navigated distribution challenges, seeking to maintain control over their product quality and shelf presence.

7. Response from Mega-Breweries

Acquisitions of Craft Breweries - Mega-breweries have responded to the craft beer movement by acquiring craft breweries, leading to debates about authenticity and independence.

Craft-Style Brands - Some mega-breweries have introduced craft-style brands to compete in the segment.

8. Craft Beer's Influence Globally

Global Craft Beer Movement - Craft beer principles have inspired similar movements worldwide, leading to the growth of craft breweries in countries beyond the United States.

Cultural Exchange - International craft brewers have embraced American craft beer styles and contributed to a global exchange of brewing techniques and flavors.

Conclusion

The craft beer movement's impact on the brewing landscape has been transformative. It has elevated beer quality and diversity, celebrated localism, and fostered a culture of innovation and consumer engagement. Craft beer has not only redefined what consumers expect from their beer but has also influenced the strategies and practices of mega-breweries. As we continue to explore, we will delve into the enduring legacy and future prospects of the craft beer movement in the brewing industry.

Conclusion

Reflecting on the Industrial Age of Brewing

In this concluding chapter, we reflect on the industrial age of brewing, a period marked by significant transformations in the beer industry. From the mechanization of brewing processes during the Industrial Revolution to the era of brewing innovations, temperance movements, and the rise of craft beer, we have journeyed through a rich tapestry of history that shaped the way we produce, consume, and appreciate beer.

The industrial age of brewing was a time of profound change, characterized by technological advancements, shifts in consumer preferences, and social movements. In this section, we take a moment to reflect on the key themes and developments that defined this era.

1. Technological Advancements

Mechanization and Efficiency - The Industrial Revolution brought mechanization to brewing, allowing for increased production, consistency, and efficiency. This era saw the introduction of new equipment like the steam engine, which revolutionized brewing processes.

Quality and Consistency - While mechanization brought benefits in terms of quantity, it also raised concerns about the quality and consistency of beer. Advances in quality control became essential to maintain consumer trust.

2. Globalization and Beer Styles

Pilsner, Lager, and Pale Lagers - The globalization of beer styles led to the dominance of pale lagers like Pilsner and Lager. These styles, with their clean and crisp profiles, became the international standard.

Exportation of British Ales - British ales, known for their robust flavors, also played a significant role in shaping global beer preferences, particularly in colonies and trading partners.

3. Temperance and Prohibition Movements

The Temperance Movement's Origins - The temperance movement emerged in response to concerns about alcohol abuse and its social consequences. It gained momentum in the 19th and early 20th centuries.

Prohibition in America - The passage of the 18th Amendment in the United States resulted in the nationwide prohibition of alcoholic beverages, profoundly impacting the brewing industry and giving rise to underground activities like bootlegging and speakeasies.

4. Brewing Innovations and Reforms

Post-Prohibition Brewing Reforms - The repeal of Prohibition in the United States brought about significant changes in brewing regulations and standards, setting the stage for the renaissance of the beer industry.

The Return of Small Breweries - Small breweries, often known as microbreweries or craft breweries, emerged, focusing on producing high-quality, distinctive beer styles.

5. Consolidation and Craft Beer Revolution

The Growth of Mega-Breweries - Consolidation within the brewing industry resulted in the emergence of mega-breweries, which employed strategies like brand diversification, price wars, and extensive distribution networks to dominate the market.

Craft Beer's Birth - The craft beer revolution was a reaction to the dominance of mega-breweries. It was driven by a desire for diversity, innovation, and the return to traditional brewing methods.

6. Craft Beer's Impact on Brewing Culture

Diverse Beer Styles and Innovation - The craft beer movement introduced a vast array of beer styles, emphasizing experimentation and innovation in brewing.

Quality and Flavor Focus - Craft brewers rekindled a focus on quality and flavor, elevating consumer expectations and promoting the use of premium ingredients.

7. Craft Beer's Enduring Legacy

Localism and Community Engagement - Craft beer celebrated local ingredients and fostered a sense of community, with breweries often serving as cultural hubs within their regions.

Economic Impact - The craft beer industry has contributed significantly to local economies, creating jobs and attracting tourism.

Global Influence - The craft beer movement inspired similar movements worldwide, encouraging the growth of craft breweries in various countries.

8. Future Prospects

Sustainability and Innovation - The future of brewing may be characterized by sustainability efforts, innovative brewing techniques, and a continued emphasis on quality and diversity.

Consumer Choice and Education - As consumers become more discerning, breweries will continue to offer a wide range of options, and education about beer styles and flavor profiles will remain essential.

Conclusion: Celebrating a Dynamic Era

The industrial age of brewing has been a dynamic and transformative era in the history of beer. It has seen the industry evolve from its humble origins to a global powerhouse, witnessed the challenges posed by temperance movements and Prohibition, and celebrated the renaissance of craft beer and the return of brewing diversity.

As we reflect on this era, it is clear that beer's history is a testament to human ingenuity, adaptability, and our enduring appreciation for the beverage that has accompanied us through millennia. The industrial age of brewing is just one chapter in this remarkable story, and the brewing landscape will continue to evolve, shaped by the tastes and preferences of generations to come. Cheers to the past, present, and future of beer!

Prohibition's Lasting Effects

In this concluding chapter, we reflect on the industrial age of brewing, a period marked by significant transformations in the beer industry. From the mechanization of brewing processes during the Industrial Revolution to the era of brewing innovations, temperance movements, and the rise of craft beer, we have journeyed through a rich tapestry of history that shaped the way we produce, consume, and appreciate beer.

One of the most defining and enduring legacies of the industrial age of brewing is the period of Prohibition in the United States and its lasting effects on the brewing industry and American culture.

1. The Passage of the 18th Amendment

Prohibition: A Social Experiment - The 18th Amendment to the U.S. Constitution, which came into effect in 1920, marked the beginning of Prohibition in the United States. It was an unprecedented attempt to ban the production, sale, and transportation of alcoholic beverages.

Underground Activities - Prohibition led to the proliferation of illegal bars known as speakeasies, bootlegging operations, and the rise of organized crime.

2. The Roaring Twenties: Bootlegging and Speakeasies

Speakeasies: Hidden Nightlife - Speakeasies were secret bars that operated during Prohibition, often requiring a password for entry. They became cultural icons of the era.

Bootlegging and Gangsters - The illegal production and distribution of alcohol led to the rise of notorious gangsters like Al Capone, who profited immensely from the illicit alcohol trade.

3. The Effects of Prohibition on Brewing Industry Workers

Lost Jobs and Businesses - The brewery industry suffered immensely during Prohibition, with many breweries closing their doors. This resulted in significant job losses for brewers and related industries.

Reinvention and Survival - Some breweries survived by pivoting to produce non-alcoholic products like soda or near beer, while others struggled to adapt.

4. Repeal and the Return of Legal Brewing

The 21st Amendment - The repeal of Prohibition came with the 21st Amendment to the U.S. Constitution in 1933, effectively ending the nationwide ban on alcohol.

Rebuilding the Brewing Industry - The repeal allowed breweries to reopen and resume legal production, though many faced challenges in rebuilding their businesses.

5. The Long-Term Impact on Brewing Culture

Corporate Consolidation - The effects of Prohibition, combined with changes in beer distribution laws, paved the way for the consolidation of the brewing industry. This eventually led to the dominance of a few mega-breweries.

Shift in Consumer Preferences - The taste for lighter, less-flavorful beer, which had gained popularity during Prohibition, persisted for decades. This preference influenced the brewing landscape for years to come.

6. Craft Beer's Response

Craft Beer's Roots - The craft beer movement, which emerged in the late 20th century, was a reaction to the dominance of mega-breweries and the desire to bring diversity, innovation, and quality back to brewing.

A Return to Tradition - Craft brewers sought to revive traditional brewing methods and reintroduce flavorful and diverse beer styles.

7. Conclusion: Navigating the Legacy of Prohibition

The era of Prohibition left an indelible mark on the brewing industry and American culture. While it initially brought about a decline in brewing and a shift in consumer preferences, it also set the stage for the resurgence of craft beer. The lasting effects of Prohibition continue to influence the brewing landscape, with craft breweries championing quality, flavor, and diversity.

As we reflect on this chapter of brewing history, we acknowledge the resilience of the industry and the enduring appeal of beer. From the shadows of Prohibition to the craft beer renaissance, the brewing world has navigated challenges and celebrated triumphs, embodying the spirit of innovation and adaptation that defines the industrial age of brewing.

The Craft Beer Movement and Beyond

In this concluding chapter, we reflect on the industrial age of brewing, a period marked by significant transformations in the beer industry. From the mechanization of brewing processes during the Industrial Revolution to the era of brewing innovations, temperance movements, and the rise of craft beer, we have journeyed through a rich tapestry of history that shaped the way we produce, consume, and appreciate beer.

The Craft Beer Movement and Beyond

As we conclude our exploration of the industrial age of brewing, we turn our attention to the craft beer movement and its enduring legacy, examining how it has not only transformed the brewing industry but also influenced the broader world of beverages and consumer culture.

1. The Birth of the Craft Beer Movement

Origins and Catalysts - The craft beer movement, which emerged in the late 20th century, was a reaction to the dominance of mega-breweries and mass-produced, flavorless beers. What were the key factors that gave birth to this movement?

Founding Principles - Craft brewers emphasized key principles such as quality, flavor, innovation, and a return to traditional brewing methods.

2. The Pioneers of Craft Beer

Key Figures - Who were the visionaries and entrepreneurs behind the early craft beer movement? We explore the stories of individuals like Fritz Maytag, Ken Grossman, Jim Koch, and Charlie Papazian.

Iconic Breweries - Iconic breweries like Sierra Nevada, Anchor Brewing, and The Boston Beer Company (Samuel Adams) played instrumental roles in shaping the movement.

3. The Craft Beer Revolution's Impact

Diverse Beer Styles and Innovation - The craft beer movement introduced an unprecedented variety of beer styles, from IPAs and stouts to sours and barrel-aged beers. How did this impact the beer landscape?

Quality and Flavor Focus - Craft brewers prioritized quality and flavor, raising consumer expectations and promoting the use of premium ingredients.

4. Localism and Community Engagement

Celebrating Local Ingredients - Craft breweries often showcased local ingredients and flavors, contributing to the resurgence of regional beer styles.

Brewery Taprooms and Brewpubs - Brewpubs and taprooms became hubs for community engagement, fostering a sense of connection between brewers and consumers.

5. Economic and Cultural Impact

Economic Growth and Job Creation - The craft beer industry has contributed significantly to local economies, creating jobs in brewing, distribution, retail, and hospitality.

Craft Beer Tourism - Craft breweries have become destinations for beer enthusiasts, attracting tourists and revenue to regions with vibrant beer scenes.

6. Craft Beer's Influence Beyond Brewing

Changing Consumer Tastes - The craft beer movement influenced consumer tastes and preferences, leading to a demand for more diverse and flavorful beverages across the alcoholic and non-alcoholic beverage industries.

Crossover with Culinary Arts - Craft beer's emphasis on flavor and innovation led to collaborations with the culinary world, inspiring chefs to incorporate beer into their creations.

7. The Global Craft Beer Movement

Craft Beer Goes Global - The craft beer movement has inspired similar movements worldwide, leading to the growth of craft breweries in countries beyond the United States.

International Collaboration - International craft brewers have embraced American craft beer styles and contributed to a global exchange of brewing techniques and flavors.

8. Craft Beer's Future Prospects

Sustainability and Innovation - The future of craft beer may be characterized by sustainability efforts, innovative brewing techniques, and a continued emphasis on quality and diversity.

Consumer Choice and Education - As consumers become more discerning, breweries will continue to offer a wide range of options, and education about beer styles and flavor profiles will remain essential.

9. Conclusion: A Legacy of Diversity and Innovation

The craft beer movement has left an indelible mark on the brewing industry and consumer culture. It has celebrated diversity, innovation, and a return to tradition. Craft brewers have championed quality, flavor, and community engagement, fostering a sense of connection between producers and consumers.

As we conclude our journey through the industrial age of brewing, we recognize the enduring legacy of the craft beer movement. It has not only revitalized the beer industry but has also influenced the way we think about and appreciate beverages in general. The spirit of the craft beer movement is a testament to the enduring human quest for quality, flavor, and connection, reminding us that the industrial age of brewing was just one chapter in the ever-evolving story of beer.

THE END

Wordbook

Welcome to the glossary section of this book. Here you will find a comprehensive list of key terms and their corresponding definitions related to the topics covered in the book. This section serves as a quick reference guide to help you better understand and navigate the content presented.

1. Beer: A fermented alcoholic beverage made from malted grains, typically barley, water, hops, and yeast.

2. Brewing: The process of producing beer, including mashing, boiling, fermenting, and conditioning.

3. Ancient Civilizations: Early human societies, such as Mesopotamia and Egypt, where the brewing of beer is believed to have originated.

4. Mesopotamia: An ancient region located between the Tigris and Euphrates rivers, often referred to as the "cradle of civilization," where the earliest evidence of beer production has been found.

5. Egypt: An ancient civilization in northeastern Africa known for its beer production and the use of beer in religious rituals.

6. Industrial Age of Brewing: The period of significant technological advancements and changes in the beer industry, including the Industrial Revolution and its impact on brewing processes.

7. Craft Beer Revolution: A movement that began in the late 20th century, characterized by the resurgence of small, independent breweries focusing on traditional brewing methods and diverse, high-quality beer styles.

8. Globalization of Beer Styles: The spread of various beer styles, such as lagers and ales, to different parts of the world due to trade and colonialism.

9. Temperance Movement: A social reform movement advocating for moderation or abstinence from alcohol consumption, which gained momentum in the 19th and early 20th centuries.

10. Prohibition: A legal ban on the production, sale, and transportation of alcoholic beverages, notably in the United States during the 1920s and early 1930s.

11. 18th Amendment: The amendment to the U.S. Constitution that prohibited the manufacture, sale, and transportation of alcoholic beverages during Prohibition.

12. Speakeasies: Illegal bars or clubs that operated during Prohibition, often requiring a secret code or password for entry.

13. Craft Brewery: A small, independent brewery that emphasizes traditional brewing methods, quality, and innovation in producing a wide range of beer styles.

14. Microbrewery: A type of craft brewery that produces beer on a smaller scale, often with a limited distribution area.

15. Brewpub: A combination of a brewery and a pub or restaurant where beer is brewed and served on-site.

16. Mega-Brewery: A large-scale brewery typically associated with multinational corporations that produce a high volume of beer.

17. Beer Marketing and Branding: Strategies and techniques used to promote and differentiate beer brands in the market.

18. Beer Variety: The diversity of beer styles, flavors, and characteristics available to consumers.

19. Beer Can: A container for holding beer, typically made of aluminum, designed for easy storage and transportation.

20. Brewing Technology: The equipment, processes, and techniques used in brewing, including advancements in fermentation and quality control.

Supplementary Materials

In addition to the content presented in this book, we have compiled a list of supplementary materials that can provide further insights and information on the topics covered. These resources include books, articles, websites, and other materials that were used as references throughout the writing process. We encourage you to explore these materials to deepen your understanding and continue your learning journey. Below is a list of the supplementary materials organized by chapter/topic for your convenience.

Introduction:

Standage, Tom. "A History of the World in 6 Glasses." Walker & Company, 2006.

Unger, Richard W. "Beer in the Middle Ages and the Renaissance." University of Pennsylvania Press, 2007.

Hornsey, Ian S. "Alcohol and Its Role in the Evolution of Human Society." Royal Society of Chemistry, 2012.

Bamforth, Charles W. "Beer: A Quality Perspective." Academic Press, 2009.

Jackson, Michael. "The New World Guide to Beer." Running Press, 1988.

Chapter 1: The Industrial Revolution and Brewing:

Mosher, Randy. "Tasting Beer: An Insider's Guide to the World's Greatest Drink." Storey Publishing, 2009.

Corran, H. S. "A History of Brewing." David & Charles, 1975.

Zainasheff, Jamil, and John J. Palmer. "Brewing Classic Styles: 80 Winning Recipes Anyone Can Brew." Brewers Publications, 2007.

Briggs, Dennis E., et al. "Brewing: Science and Practice." CRC Press, 2004.

Bamforth, Charles W. "Beer: Tap into the Art and Science of Brewing." Oxford University Press, 2003.

Chapter 2: The Globalization of Beer Styles:

Papazian, Charlie. "The Complete Joy of Homebrewing." William Morrow Paperbacks, 2014.

Daniels, Ray. "Designing Great Beers: The Ultimate Guide to Brewing Classic Beer Styles." Brewers Publications, 2000.

Alworth, Jeff. "The Beer Bible." Workman Publishing Company, 2015.

Cornell, Martyn. "Amber, Gold & Black: The History of Britain's Great Beers." The History Press, 2010.

Oliver, Garrett. "The Brewmaster's Table: Discovering the Pleasures of Real Beer with Real Food." HarperCollins, 2003.

Chapter 3: Temperance and the Road to Prohibition:

Rorabaugh, W. J. "The Alcoholic Republic: An American Tradition." Oxford University Press, 1979.

Okrent, Daniel. "Last Call: The Rise and Fall of Prohibition." Scribner, 2010.

Blocker, Jack S., et al. "Alcohol and Temperance in Modern History: An International Encyclopedia." ABC-CLIO, 2003.

Pegram, Thomas R. "Battling Demon Rum: The Struggle for a Dry America, 1800-1933." Ivan R. Dee, 1998.

Lender, Mark Edward, and James Kirby Martin. "Drinking in America: A History." Free Press, 1982.

Chapter 4: Prohibition in America:

Kobler, John. "Ardent Spirits: The Rise and Fall of Prohibition." Da Capo Press, 1993.

Kyvig, David E. "Repealing National Prohibition." University of Chicago Press, 1979.

Okrent, Daniel. "Last Call: The Rise and Fall of Prohibition." Scribner, 2010.

Lerner, Michael A., and Scott Martin. "Brewing Battles: A History of American Beer." Algora Publishing, 2007.

Sinclair, Andrew. "Prohibition: The Era of Excess." Little, Brown and Company, 1962.

Chapter 5: Brewing Innovations and the Rebirth of Beer:

Alworth, Jeff. "The Beer Bible." Workman Publishing Company, 2015.

Papazian, Charlie. "The Complete Joy of Homebrewing." William Morrow Paperbacks, 2014.

Bamforth, Charles W. "Beer Is Proof God Loves Us: Reaching for the Soul of Beer and Brewing." FT Press, 2010.

Miller, Dave. "The Complete Handbook of Home Brewing." Storey Publishing, 1992.

Noonan, Gregory J. "New Brewing Lager Beer: The Most Comprehensive Book for Home-and Microbrewers." Brewers Publications, 1996.

Chapter 6: Consolidation and the Rise of Beer Giants:

Unger, Richard W. "Beer in the Middle Ages and the Renaissance." University of Pennsylvania Press, 2007.

DeBenedetti, Christian. "The Great American Ale Trail: The Craft Beer Lover's Guide to the Best Watering Holes in the Nation." Running Press, 2011.

Bamforth, Charles W. "Beer: A Quality Perspective." Academic Press, 2009.

Nelson, Max. "The Barbarian's Beverage: A History of Beer in Ancient Europe." Routledge, 2005.

Jackson, Michael. "The World Guide to Beer." Running Press, 2009.

Chapter 7: The Craft Beer Revolution:

Alworth, Jeff. "The Beer Bible." Workman Publishing Company, 2015.

Daniels, Ray. "Designing Great Beers: The Ultimate Guide to Brewing Classic Beer Styles." Brewers Publications

www.ingramcontent.com/pod-product-compliance
Lightning Source LLC
LaVergne TN
LVHW012109070526
838202LV00056B/5676